The Resource Book
A Teacher's Tool Kit

to accompany

Adolescence:
Continuity, Change, and Diversity
Second Edition

Nancy J. Cobb
California State University, Los Angeles

Separate computerized and printed Test Bank available to adopters upon request.
Test Bank prepared by Andrea Weyerman, Augusta College, Georgia.

Mayfield Publishing Company
Mountain View, California
London • Toronto

Manufactured in the United States of America
10 9 8 7 6 5 4 3 2 1

Mayfield Publishing Company
1280 Villa Street
Mountain View, California 94041

PREFACE

As I thought about what you should know about this Resource Book, a number of things came to mind. In the end, they all came down to one single point: This Resource Book is simply here to make it easier for you to teach the course.

Many things could be included in a guide such as this; however, if they all were, it would be difficult to find what you wanted when you needed it. In deciding what to include, one question served as a guideline: "How useful will this material be?" Usefulness in this case refers either to presenting a new way of teaching a concept or enhancing the way material might already be taught.

To avoid some of the difficulties I have experienced with other resource guides, I have kept the organization of this one simple. Information is organized in two distinct sections, Part I and Part II. The first part contains information of a general nature that should be useful throughout the course; the second contains information specific to each chapter.

Part I of the Resource Book begins with information and materials helpful in preparing the course, such as the Course Planner/Calendar, advice on how to adapt the text to alternative organizations (either topical or chronological) and tables comparing information in this textbook with seven other adolescent texts. Part I continues with a section on methods for involving students, including lists of class activities and worksheets and guidelines for conducting group discussions and using student journals. In addition, four handouts are included to help students with their reading, writing, and observational skills throughout the course and to help you in conducting group discussions in class. These may be found in the Handouts and Transparency Masters section in Part I along with a list of nearly seventy transparency masters to make your lectures more dynamic. Finally, bibliographies of general and gender- and ethnicity-specific books, articles, journals, and periodicals may be found toward the end of Part I, along with information on viewing films about adolescence and networking on the information highway—all to aid you in your general course preparation.

Part II presents ancillary materials for each chapter of the text, including chapter outlines, key terms, and learning objectives, along with the class activities and worksheets listed in Part I. Finally, suggested readings and audiovisuals to excite class discussion and support your lecture presentation are listed in each chapter. The transparency masters listed in Part I have been compiled at the back of the Resource Book.

The Test Bank, an important part of these teaching support materials, has been prepared as a separate printed and computerized volume for easier use. The questions that appear in the Test Bank are also available in Mayfield's Academic Management Software package designed for IBM-compatible and Macintosh computers.

A set of films on adolescence is available through Mayfield to adopters of the text.

The staff at Mayfield Publishing is available to assist you should you encounter any difficulties or have any questions. You can call your Mayfield representative or reach the publisher directly at 800-433-1279.

Finally, I am interested in any comments you may have on materials in this Resource Book or the text itself. You can reach me at the Psychology Department; California State University, Los Angeles; 5151 State University Drive; Los Angeles, California 90032.

Nancy Cobb

CONTENTS

PART I

General Course Preparation

COURSE PLANNER/CALENDAR

Use this Course Planner/Calendar to organize lecture material, class activities, and dates for films and videos. This calendar can facilitate scheduling guest speakers and ordering films and videos and can serve as a reminder to photocopy materials to be distributed in class.

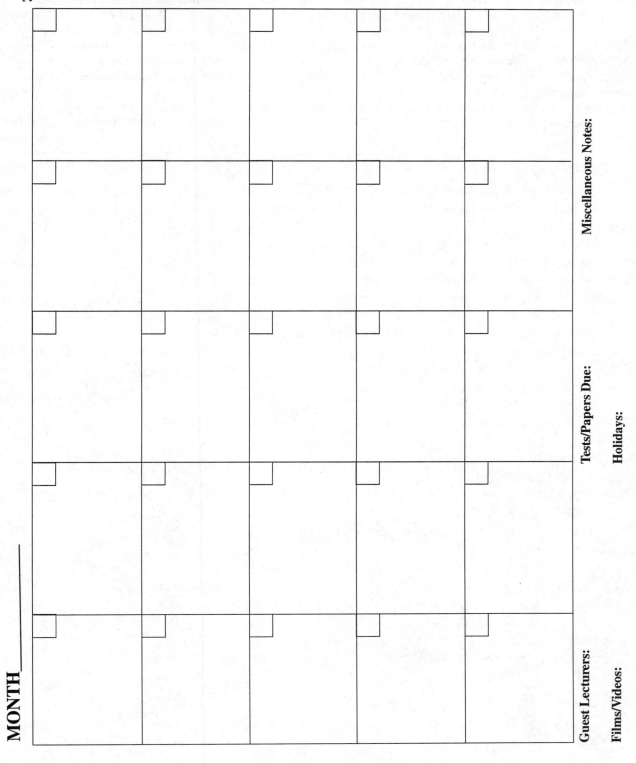

MONTH _____

Miscellaneous Notes:

Tests/Papers Due:

Holidays:

Guest Lecturers:

Films/Videos:

ADAPTING THE TEXT TO ALTERNATIVE ORGANIZATIONS

Because of the modular nature of this text, it is easily adapted to either a strictly chronological or a strictly topical approach. Presently it combines the two approaches. Material is presented in three sections, or modules. The first is similar to that of many other texts in the field, covering introductory material and developmental theories. The second and third sections of the text divide the study of adolescence into two chronological periods. The first covers early adolescence, examining the biological, cognitive and social-emotional foundations of adolescent development. The second section covers late adolescence, beginning with a chapter on identity and continuing with three subsequent chapters, each of which considers a separate aspect of identity: sexuality and adult gender-roles, work and college, and the development of values and beliefs. The last two chapters cover atypical development and research methods and issues.

I hope that you will find the existing framework of the text preferable to either a strictly topical or a strictly chronological organization. It is, however, easily adapted to fit either. The outline below shows how chapters can be organized into a strictly topical approach.

Theoretical Foundations
> Chapter 1: A Lifespan Perspective on Adolescence
> Chapter 2: Theoretical Foundations of Adolescent Development

Research Methods and Issues
> Chapter 13: Studying Adolescence: Research Methods and Issues
> Research Focus Boxes

Biological Development and Puberty
> Chapter 3: The Biological Context of Development: Puberty

Cognitive Development
> Chapter 4: Cognitive Development: Processes and Transitions
> Chapter 10: Careers and College
> Chapter 11: Facing the Future: Values in Transition

Social and Emotional Development
> Chapter 6: Adolescents and Their Friends
> Chapter 5: Adolescents in the Family

Personality Development
> Chapter 8: Defining the Self: Identity and Intimacy
> Chapter 5: Adolescents in the Family

Sexual Development
> Chapter 9: The Sexual Self
> Chapter 3: The Biological Context of Development: Puberty

Atypical Development
> Chapter 12: Atypical Development

Educational Development
> Chapter 7: Adolescents in the Schools
> Chapter 10: Careers and College

Career Development
> Chapter 10: Careers and College

TEXTBOOK COMPARISONS

When selecting a textbook for your course in adolescent development, you have a wide selection of current textbooks from which to choose. In some key respects all texts have certain things in common: The organization of the subject is surprisingly recognizable from one textbook to another, and a common core of classic and contemporary research on essential topics is likely to be represented in all of the textbooks under consideration. Important differences remain, however, and these can subtly but profoundly affect the success of a text in your course.

This brief comparative summary of seven standard works in adolescent development against the new edition of *Adolescence: Continuity, Change, and Diversity,* Second Edition, will help you identify the key features that distinguish this book from other textbooks in adolescent development. By referring to the chapter by chapter comparisons with these texts that are outlined on the following pages, you will find many points of similarity and of difference in organization that will be helpful in making the changes and adjustments to your course. Brief remarks regarding theme, organization, and depth of coverage appear at the beginning of each textbook comparison.

Whatever the differences in how this textbook is organized and the implications of these to the way you teach the course, there are three overriding features to consider when comparing *Adolescence: Continuity, Change, and Diversity* to any other textbook. They are: integrative emphases, thematic organization, and the development of theory and research content throughout. These three distinguishing features provide a rich and intensely interesting exploration of adolescent development and psychology.

First, the integrative emphases found throughout this work include in-depth discussions of gender differences and similarities, real or imagined, that deeply affect the development of individual adolescents. The same in-depth focus is given to ethnic and cultural differences that are only now becoming widely recognized and accepted as significant and fundamental to understanding adolescents. You will notice that some textbooks still attempt to isolate and cover such fundamental content and issues within discrete chapters. The approach in *Adolescence: Continuity, Change, and Diversity* is, therefore, a departure.

Second, the organization of this textbook stresses the roles of continuity and change as they affect adolescents' development from the inner contexts of experience (biological/pubertal changes, cognitive development, and the role of peers, family, and schooling) to the outer contexts of identity, personality consolidation, and intimacy. Throughout, the text reminds students of the differences between the challenges and contexts of early and late adolescents' lives. Also, this book is distinctive in its attention to theory and examples that present adolescence within the perspective of lifespan development.

Finally, the text anchors students' developing knowledge of adolescence to a solid research base by integrating discussions of research methods and design into each chapter in the form of research focus boxes. Other texts in adolescent development isolate the research concerns and applications to a single chapter.

Adolescence and Youth, 4th Edition
John J. Conger
©1991, Harper/Collins

Conger gives greater emphasis to family and parenting issues and to social concerns, such as the problems of drugs, alienation, delinquency, and psychological problems more than developmental issues per se. Conger is the only comparison text that does not devote a chapter to identity formation and development. Nor does it include a chapter on research methods and issues, or integrate discussion of research into each chapter.

Cobb, 720 pages	Conger, 697 pages
Ch. 1: A Lifespan Perspective on Adolescence	Ch. 1: A New Generation: History, Issues, Stage Development
Ch. 2: Theoretical Foundations of Adolescent Development	Ch. 2: Viewing Development: Change and Challenge (Concepts)
Ch. 3: The Biological Context of Development: Puberty	Ch. 3: Biological Changes in Adolescence
Ch. 4: Cognitive Development: Processes and Transitions	Ch. 4: Intelligence and Cognitive Development
Ch. 5: Adolescents in the Family	Ch. 5: Adolescents, Families, and Social Change Ch. 6: Parent-Child Relations and Adolescent Development
Ch. 6: Adolescents and Their Friends	Ch. 8: Adolescents and their Peers
Ch. 7: Adolescents in the Schools	Ch. 9: Adolescents and the Schools
Ch. 8: Defining the Self: Identity and Intimacy	
Ch. 9: The Sexual Self: Close Relationships in Late Adolescence	Ch. 7: Adolescent Sexuality
Ch. 10: Careers and College	Ch. 10: Vocational Choice in a Changing World
Ch. 11: Facing the Future: Values in Transition	Ch. 12: Moral Development and Values
Ch. 12: Atypical Development in Adolescence	Ch. 11: Adolescents and Drugs Ch. 13: Alienation and Delinquency Ch. 14: Psychological and Psychophysiological Disturbance in Adolescence
Ch. 13: Studying Adolescence: Research Methods and Issues	

Adolescent Development

John Dacey/Maureen Kenney
©1994, Brown/Benchmark

The Dacey and Kenny textbook emphasizes applied and multicultural content relative to developmental issues per se. For instance, schooling and work are collapsed into a single chapter and three chapters are devoted to non-normative development. Research methods and issues are not treated in detail.

Cobb, 720 pages	**Dacey/Kenny,** 520 pages
Ch. 1: A Lifespan Perspective on Adolescence	Ch. 1: What Is Adolescence?
Ch. 2: Theoretical Foundations of Adolescent Development	Ch. 2: General Theories of Adolescence: An Overview
Ch. 3: The Biological Context of Development: Puberty	Ch. 3: Physical Development
Ch. 4: Cognitive Development: Processes and Transitions	Ch. 4: Cognitive Development
Ch. 5: Adolescents in the Family	Ch. 7: Family Relations
Ch. 6: Adolescents and Their Friends	Ch. 8: Social Relations
Ch. 7: Adolescents in the Schools	Ch. 10: Education and Work
Ch. 8: Defining the Self: Identity and Intimacy	Ch. 6: The Self and Identity Formation
Ch. 9: The Sexual Self: Close Relationships in Late Adolescence	Ch. 9: Sexuality
Ch. 10: Careers and College	
Ch. 11: Facing the Future: Values in Transition	Ch. 5: Morality and Spirituality
Ch. 12: Atypical Development in Adolescence	Ch. 11: Stress and Mental Disturbance
	Ch. 12: Substance Abuse
	Ch. 13: Delinquent Behavior
Ch. 13: Studying Adolescence: Research Methods and Issues	
	Ch. 14: Initiation and Adulthood

Adolescent Development and Behavior, 2nd Edition
Jerome Dusek
©1991, Prentice-Hall

Dusek's textbook places somewhat greater emphasis on raising adolescents than understanding adolescent development.

Cobb, 720 pages	**Dusek,** 480 pages
Ch. 1: A Lifespan Perspective on Adolescence	Ch. 1: Introduction to Adolescence
Ch. 2: Theoretical Foundations of Adolescent Development	Ch. 2: Theories of Adolescence
Ch. 3: The Biological Context of Development: Puberty	Ch. 3: Biological Change and Adolescent Development
Ch. 4: Cognitive Development: Processes and Transitions	Ch. 4: Intellectual and Cognitive Development in Adolescence
Ch. 5: Adolescents in the Family	Ch. 10: Parent and Family Influences on Adolescent Socialization
Ch. 6: Adolescents and Their Friends	Ch. 11: Peer-Group Influences on Adolescent Development
Ch. 7: Adolescents in the Schools	Ch. 12: School Influences on Adolescent Development
Ch. 8: Defining the Self: Identity and Intimacy	Ch. 6: Self-Concept, Self-Esteem, and Identity
Ch. 9: The Sexual Self: Close Relationships in Late Adolescence	Ch. 7: Sex-Role Socialization Ch. 8: Adolescent Sexuality
Ch. 10: Careers and College	Ch. 9: Vocational Development
Ch. 11: Facing the Future: Values in Transition	Ch. 5: Moral Development in Adolescence
Ch. 12: Atypical Development in Adolescence	Ch. 13: Deviant Behavior During Adolescence
Ch. 13: Studying Adolescence: Research Methods and Issues	Appendix: Methods of Research in the Study of Adolescence

The Adolescent, 7th Edition

F. Philip Rice
©1992, Allyn/Bacon

Rice's textbook, though approximately the same length as Cobb's, is organized into seven parts and twenty-one chapters. Considerable emphasis is placed on parenting issues (three chapters) and on problems of adolescent development. Gender is treated as an isolated topic.

Cobb, 720 pages	**Rice,** 580 pages
Ch. 1: A Lifespan Perspective on Adolescence	Ch. 1: Profiles of Adolescents in Contemporary Society Ch. 2: Cultural Diversity
Ch. 2: Theoretical Foundations of Adolescent Development	Ch. 3: Multidisciplinary Views of Adolescence
Ch. 3: The Biological Context of Development: Puberty	Ch. 7: Sexual Maturation and Physical Growth Ch. 8: The Body Image
Ch. 4: Cognitive Development: Processes and Transitions	Ch. 9: Cognitive Growth and Change Ch. 10: Intelligence, Information Processing, and Decision Making
Ch. 5: Adolescents in the Family	Ch. 4: Adolescents in Their Families Ch. 5: Divorced, Parent-Abused, and Blended Families Ch. 6: Functional versus Dysfunctional Families
Ch. 6: Adolescents and Their Friends	
Ch. 7: Adolescents in the Schools	Ch. 20: Education and School
Ch. 8: Defining the Self: Identity and Intimacy	Ch. 11: Self-Concept, Self Esteem, and Identity Status
Ch. 9: The Sexual Self: Close Relationships in Late Adolescence	Ch. 15: Gender Identity and Gender Roles Ch. 16: Sexual Values, Behavior, and Education Ch. 18: Social Development, Relationships, Dating, Nonmarital Cohabitation, and Marriage
Ch. 10: Careers and College	Ch. 21: Work and Vocation
Ch. 11: Facing the Future: Values in Transition	Ch. 17: Adolescent Society, Culture, and Subculture Ch. 19: The Development of Moral Judgment, Character, Values, Beliefs, and Behavior
Ch. 12: Atypical Development in Adolescence	Ch. 12: Stress and Emotional Disorders Ch. 13: Adolescent Alienation Ch. 14: Substance Abuse, Addiction, and Dependency
Ch. 13: Studying Adolescence: Research Methods and Issues	

Adolescence and Youth, **4th Edition**
John Santrock
©1993, Brown/Benchmark

The similarities in general organization and sequencing between Cobb and Santrock are strong. The biggest difference is in Cobb's emphasis on gender and ethnic and cultural differences and in their integration throughout each chapter. Santrock tends to treat such topics in isolated content (boxes) or as a separate chapter (11). Cobb also provides a chapter on research and methods and integrates a discussion of research into each chapter through the use of research focus boxes. Santrock gives more emphasis to problems that commonly appear in late adolescence (Chapters 11, 12, and 13).

Cobb, 720 pages	**Santrock,** 688 pages
Ch. 1: A Lifespan Perspective on Adolescence	Ch. 1: Introduction: The Nature of Adolescent Development
Ch. 2: Theoretical Foundations of Adolescent Development	Ch. 2: Theories and Methods
Ch. 3: The Biological Context of Development: Puberty	Ch. 3: Biological Processes and Physical Development
Ch. 4: Cognitive Development: Processes and Transitions	Ch. 4: Cognitive Development and Social Cognition Ch. 5: Information Processing and Intelligence
Ch. 5: Adolescents in the Family	Ch. 6: Families
Ch. 6: Adolescents and Their Friends	Ch. 7: Peers
Ch. 7: Adolescents in the Schools	Ch. 8: Schools Ch. 9: Culture
Ch. 8: Defining the Self: Identity and Intimacy	Ch. 10: The Self and Identity Ch. 11: Gender
Ch. 9: The Sexual Self: Close Relationships in Late Adolescence	Ch. 12: Sexuality
Ch. 10: Careers and College	Ch. 14: Achievement, Work, and Careers
Ch. 11: Facing the Future: Values in Transition	Ch. 13: Moral Development, Values, and Religion
Ch. 12: Atypical Development in Adolescence	Ch. 15: Problems and Disturbances Ch. 16: Stress and Health
Ch. 13: Studying Adolescence: Research Methods and Issues	

Adolescent Psychology: A Developmental View, 2nd Edition

Norman A. Sprinthall/W. Andrew Collins
©1988, McGraw-Hill

Sprinthall and Collins offer a thoughtful, but somewhat dated, analysis of adolescent development. Issues of diversity are not emphasized as much as in Cobb's text, and a chapter on research is not included.

Cobb, 720 pages	Sprinthall/Collins, 576 pages
Ch. 1: A Lifespan Perspective on Adolescence	Ch. 1: History and Directing Concepts
Ch. 2: Theoretical Foundations of Adolescent Development	
Ch. 3: The Biological Context of Development: Puberty	Ch. 2: Physical Changes and Their Psychological Effects
Ch. 4: Cognitive Development: Processes and Transitions	Ch. 3: Cognitive Growth Ch. 4: Social Reasoning
Ch. 5: Adolescents in the Family	Ch. 7: Family Relations and Influences
Ch. 6: Adolescents and Their Friends	Ch. 8: Peer Relations and Influences
Ch. 7: Adolescents in the Schools	Ch. 12: Adolescents and Secondary Schools
Ch. 8: Defining the Self: Identity and Intimacy	Ch. 5: Adolescence and Identity Formation
Ch. 9: The Sexual Self: Close Relationships in Late Adolescence	Ch. 9: Adolescent Sexuality
Ch. 10: Careers and College	Ch. 13: Career Development Ch. 14: College Students: A New Phase of Adolescence?
Ch. 11: Facing the Future: Values in Transition	Ch. 6: Moral Judgment and Value Development
Ch. 12: Atypical Development in Adolescence	Ch. 10: Juvenile Delinquency Ch. 11: Psychological Disturbance and Alienation
Ch. 13: Studying Adolescence: Research Methods and Issues	

Adolescence, 3rd Edition
Laurence Steinberg
©1993, McGraw-Hill

Steinberg's textbook emphasizes the context in which adolescents live (families, peers, schools, and work). The organization moves from the fundamentals of biological and social development to these contexts and to dimensions of psychosocial development. Cobb's organization is similar but gives greater emphasis to the role of gender in adolescent development and to cultural differences.

Cobb, 720 pages	**Steinberg,** 540 pages
Ch. 1: A Lifespan Perspective on Adolescence	
Ch. 2: Theoretical Foundations of Adolescent Development	
Ch. 3: The Biological Context of Development: Puberty	Ch. 1: Biological Transitions
Ch. 4: Cognitive Development: Processes and Transitions	Ch. 2: Cognitive Transitions Ch. 3: Social Transitions
Ch. 5: Adolescents in the Family	Ch. 4: Families
Ch. 6: Adolescents and Their Friends	Ch. 5: Peer Groups
Ch. 7: Adolescents in the Schools	Ch. 6: Schools
Ch. 8: Defining the Self: Identity and Intimacy	Ch. 8: Identity
Ch. 9: The Sexual Self: Close Relationships in Late Adolescence	Ch. 10: Intimacy Ch. 11: Sexuality
Ch. 10: Careers and College	Ch. 7: Work and Leisure Ch. 12: Achievement
Ch. 11: Facing the Future: Values in Transition	Ch. 9: Autonomy
Ch. 12: Atypical Development in Adolescence	Ch. 13: Psychosocial Problems in Adolescence
Ch. 13: Studying Adolescence: Research Methods and Issues	

GUIDELINES FOR CONDUCTING GROUP DISCUSSIONS

By Michael Wapner

Group discussions can be effective and welcome as an occasional change of pace from a lecture format or as a more regular and integral part of the course. Central to success in both cases is the establishment of: (a) sufficiently clear goal(s) to focus discussion and (b) a structure that will both guide students and make it safe for them to participate.

A. Goals:

1. To get to know and feel comfortable with other members of the class.

2. To work cooperatively toward arriving at some consensus or definition of differences that might then be reported to the larger class or serve as the basis for a written report.

3. To exchange personal experiences that will further an appreciation of gender, ethnic, age, and other differences.

4. To allow students to explore their own experiences.

B. Structure:

Each of these goals is a worthy and useful focus for group discussion. But each is different from the others in some significant way and thus requires a somewhat different structure.

1. Large lecture classes are often cold and impersonal and for some students inhibit even the minimal participation of asking a question or volunteering a comment. A single group discussion early in the course either among all the students (difficult in very large classes) or within smaller subgroups can go a long way toward breaking the ice. In this case, asking the group a simple question, such as "What was the most difficult (interesting, surprising, enjoyable) aspect of your own adolescence?" will elicit a relatively brief but moderately personal response from a variety of students. Students should be encouraged to keep answers short. The structure can be loose and humorous. Sarcastic or ironic contributions are welcome because laughter and out-of-turn comments reduce inhibitions and make future participation easier.

2. Discussions which must result in some product require an explicit statement of their purpose. Students will need help to achieve that end. Personal issues and agendas must be set aside, and the responsibilities of the participants must be defined. Generally, such groups will find it necessary to meet a number of times to achieve their purpose, and the result is often a stronger connection among the group members and weaker relations between the group and the rest of the class. Once started, these groups can work independently, often outside of class.

3. The discussion of personal experiences to further the understanding of racial, ethnic, gender, or generational differences is best conducted in small groups (not larger than seven or eight students). Students should be helped to not criticize or comment negatively on the experiences of others. These discussions run more smoothly when a leader is designated who can control the allotment of time and make sure everyone who wishes to has the opportunity to participate. Students should be helped to hear, acknowledge, and discuss the experiences of others and to resist simply waiting to report their own.

4. Exploring one's own experience is different from simply reporting it. This is the most sensitive but also the most educationally powerful of the types of discussion mentioned here. Many of the developmental changes discussed in the text have been negotiated by some students with difficulty, and those students may experience some tension in reading about or discussing these. Although the classroom is not a context for psychotherapy, the reconsideration and clarification of one's own experience is, for some instructors, a legitimate educational goal. It also may happen that a student in a group that has been convened for the third purpose begins to speak of an experience in a deeper way that the instructor does not wish to end abruptly.It is important that the student who is speaking not disclose more—in

retrospect—than will be comfortable. The instructor can help prevent this by gently interrupting with a comment like, "What you are discussing seems pretty personal; you can stop if you want." Should the student continue, the student should be given more time than in any of the above groups to talk about this experience. It is not essential that everyone in the group explore her or his own experience, but it is important that more than one do so, lest the one student feel singularly exposed. The participation of the other members of the group tends to be more supportive in this case, helping, with questions and short comments, the speaker place the experience within the context of the course material.

USE OF STUDENT JOURNALS

By Michael Wapner

Having students keep a journal in which they make regular entries is a particularly appropriate exercise for a developmental class since it documents actual growth over the period of the course. There are different kinds of journals, but I have found what I call a "problem-focused" journal to be particularly useful. In this type of journal, the student focuses on what she or he finds problematic in lectures, readings, or any other portion of the class material. Entries such as the following should be encouraged:

> Instructor lectured today about developmental stages. I don't get it. How do you know when one stage ends and another begins? I don't remember changing stages.

The first benefit of such an entry is obvious. It serves to crystallize a question which can then be asked in class or researched. A follow-up entry might read:

> Oh, now I get it. A change of stage is a kind of break where you stop doing things the old way. I remember when I started not wanting my mother to clean my room. It was at the same time that I started wanting to shop for my own clothes.

This second entry both makes explicit an important concept in the course but also displays to the student the development of her own understanding. It is common for an insight such as the one above to trigger other discoveries, and one finds that journal entries cluster with related insights. Documenting the growth of one's own understanding is wonderfully motivating.

Students should be encouraged to write something in the journal every day or, at the last, following every class meeting and/or study session. Keeping a journal is a habit that must be cultivated, like brushing one's teeth. Thus some entries may be superficial or downright silly (for example, "Read three pages of text just now. Didn't understand a thing. I'll try again later."). Such entries should not be criticized or graded down. It is counterproductive for the student to be too careful about the quality of entries. I have found it most workable not to grade journals at all; I simply require them to be handed in twice during the semester. I write as many supportive comments as I have time for and grade them Credit/No Credit based on the number of entries and their overall thoughtfulness.

CLASS ACTIVITIES

The individual chapter materials in Part II of the resource book include the following class activities.

Chapter 1   A Lifespan Perspective on Adolescence

    1-1   Cultural Stereotypes of Adolescents
    1-2   Interviewing Adolescents
    1-3   Adolescents Today and Yesterday
    1-4   Generating a Stereotype

Chapter 2   Theoretical Foundations of Adolescent Development

    2-1   A Theoretical Cocktail Party
    2-2   Problem Solving
    2-3   Advice Columns

Chapter 3   The Biological Context of Development: Puberty

    3-1   Keeping a Journal
    3-2   Reactions to Menarche/Spermarche
    3-3   Role-Playing a Parental Discussion About Sex
    3-4   Media Portrayal of Adolescent Sexuality

Chapter 4   Cognitive Development: Processes and Transitions

    4-1   The Development of Humor
    4-2   Demonstrating Logical Thinking

Chapter 5   Adolescents in the Family

    5-1   Media Portrayal of Family Conflict
    5-2   Cultural Stereotypes of Family Roles
    5-3   Role-Playing Active Listening
    5-4   Role-Playing Styles of Parenting

Chapter 6   Adolescents and Their Friends

    6-1   Analysis of Popular Music Lyrics
    6-2   Naturalistic Observation: Teen Language
    6-3   High School Crowds
    6-4   Friendship Survey

Chapter 7   Adolescents in the Schools

    7-1   Visiting a High School
    7-2   Survey of Homework and Television

Chapter 8   Defining the Self: Identity and Intimacy

    8-1   Role-Playing Identity Statuses
    8-2   Cultural Images of Ethnicity
    8-3   Small Group Discussions of Self-Concept in Adulthood and Adolescence
    8-4   Perspectives on Maturity

STUDENT WORKSHEETS

The individual chapter materials in Part II of the resource book include the following worksheets to accompany class activities.

SQ4R—OR HOW TO READ YOUR TEXTBOOK

Reading a textbook usually isn't a problem—it's remembering what you have read afterwards that's difficult. SQ4R is an approach to reading a textbook that will help you better remember what you have read. At the heart of this approach is a well-known fact: We remember things best when we understand them and when they are meaningful to us. When what we are reading doesn't make sense or has no meaning we are forced to remember it by rote—by simply memorizing it. SQ4R is a way of making the text meaningful, thereby allowing you to remember what you have read rather than forcing you to rely on memorization.

The SQ4R approach is a skill, and it takes time to master. Once you have mastered this approach, however, it will take you less time to read the text than it did without using this method. An analogy to roller skating may help here. If you don't know how to roller skate, getting from one place to another on skates will take much longer and will be more difficult than simply walking. However, once you know how to skate, skating will be much faster than walking.

SQ4R is an acronym for a six-step approach to reading: Survey-Question-Read-Reflect-Recite-Review.

Step 1: Survey

The first step in reading a chapter is to get a sense of how the chapter is organized, of how the different pieces fit together. The first place to start when surveying the chapter is with the outline. How many major sections is the chapter divided into? Is there a logical order to these? Most of the chapters in this text are organized into about five sections. You can identify chapter sections by the type; the headings are typed in uppercase letters.

Once you have looked at the organization of the chapter, begin to survey the first section. Surveying may be the hardest step in this procedure because it requires you to break a well learned habit. When you survey, you are literally to flip through the pages *without reading them.* You are looking for the key points; these appear as italicized terms or subheads in bold type.

Step 2: Question

Many of the terms and headings that emerge in the survey will have no meaning at first. This is actually an advantage for you since one of the purposes of the survey is to get you to formulate questions which you can then answer as you read. Posing questions about the material allows you to transform your reading of the chapter from a passive to an active process. When you actively read material, as you do when you put it to some use (for example, by answering the questions you generated), you remember the material better. Another metaphor might help here. Passive reading is like "straightening up" a room when there isn't time to actually put things away. One simply opens the closet door and tosses everything in. Of course, things end up in a jumble at the bottom of the closet, and it is impossible later to find what you want. The questions you formulate in the survey step provide mental hooks on which to "hang" the information that you are tossing into memory, making it easier to retrieve the information you need.

Step 3: Read

This step may sound familiar but there's a catch to it. You need first to determine how many pages you can read at a sitting before your attention begins to wander. A common measure of wandering is "page turning." Be honest with yourself at this point. It's no good telling yourself that you can read twelve pages when all you can read without getting the jitters or nodding off is three. There is a reason why honesty is important: You can only attend to one thing at a time, and for something to be adequately encoded into memory you must attend to it. Only read a section that is no longer than one you can give your undivided attention to.

Step 4: Reflect

After reading the section, put the book aside and take a moment to reflect on what you have read. What was the general sense of this passage? Of your own experiences, which can you relate to what you have read? In other words, can you personalize this information?

Step 5:   Recite

Keeping the book closed, recite what you have just read. One way to rehearse is to say the information out loud. Another is to jot down the main points on paper. You may want to combine these approaches by writing out key terms and headings and then verbally reciting what you remember of them.

Step 6:   Review

After reciting what you have read, open the book and review the material, checking to see what you correctly recalled and what you need to read again. When you have gone through each of the sections of the chapter this way, go back once more and review the chapter as a whole.

READING A JOURNAL ARTICLE

Reading a journal article can be a formidable task to the uninitiated, with page after page of technical terms, methodological procedures, statistics, and a discussion summing it all up that, in some articles, can make watching grass grow seem exciting by comparison. There are people who enjoy sitting down with a good journal article, as others do with a good book (your professor is probably one of these), but for the novice the seductive qualities of a scientific paper can be easy to miss. As with other fields of expertise, the more one knows about the area, the more fascinating it becomes. You will not become an expert after reading this handout, but you will be able to read a scientific paper more easily, leaving you more time to think about it and to begin to pull things together.

Where should you begin? Answers such as "At the beginning" are not much help and are not always the best advice. Journal articles, like major appliances and toys to assemble at holidays, should come with a set of instructions. Since they don't, the following remarks should serve to orient you to the task.

Step 1:   Getting an Overview

The **Abstract,** the paragraph immediately beneath the byline, is the closest thing to instructions that you will get. This paragraph summarizes the entire article, indicating what the investigators hoped to find, how they collected their data, what they actually found, and how they interpreted their findings. Because the Abstract gives an overview of the article, it is a good place to start. Even before this, however, a quick glance at the **Title** will usually tell you what the research was about, because the title mentions by name each variable that was studied; for example, "Effects of paternal absence on sex-typed behavior . . . ." "Individual differences in cheating," "Parental conflict and adolescent rebellion."

Step 2:   Scan, Don't Read

Before reading the article itself, it's a good idea to quickly scan each section to see the type of information each contains. A research article has five sections: Abstract, Introduction, Method, Results, and Discussion. Glance at the opening section, the Introduction; it is organized around the variables that were investigated, reviewing findings first for one, then the other. After reading about each variable, you should begin to get an idea of where the research is headed. Can you ask questions that could be rephrased as hypotheses at the end of the Introduction? Researchers phrase the questions that prompted their research, as hypotheses. Scan the Method section to see the type of research that was conducted. Was it an experiment? A correlational study? A naturalistic observation? What were the subjects' ages? How were the data collected? Did subjects fill out a questionnaire? Were they interviewed? Did the investigators observe their behavior directly? Look briefly at the Results section. How were the data analyzed? Now go to the Discussion section. What types of conclusions did the investigators reach? Finally, check the references. Are they current?

Step 3:   Reading the Article

Once you have scanned the article, you can start reading. Go back to the **Introduction.** The Introduction is organized in three parts. The first of these introduces the reader to the problem that was studied. This part is very brief, a sentence or two, and opens this section. The main body of the Introduction follows, usually with no noticeable break, and reviews theory and past research that are related to the variables being investigated. After reading this part of the Introduction, you are ready for the hypotheses that the investigators have formulated, the third and final part of the Introduction. Hypotheses are statements concerning relationships among the variables being studied—what the investigators expected to find.

The **Method** section is next. This section is divided into several subsections. The first of these, on "subjects," tells you the type of subjects that were studied. It gives information about their age, sex, and other characteristics such as ethnicity, family income level, and so on. A "procedure" subsection describes how the data were collected, the tests and measures that were used, and the conditions that subjects experienced. It also states the type of research design used (for example, whether subjects in different conditions were matched, whether all subjects experienced all conditions, and so on).

The **Results** section usually opens with summary statistics, such as means, for the different conditions. A description of the tests of significance that were used to evaluate differences among these follows. This section can be easy for some students to follow and impossible for others depending on their familiarity with the statistics that are commonly used in developmental research. For those who have a familiarity, statistical tests offer meaningful short hand ways of summarizing research findings. Those without such a familiarity can refer to the Discussion section to determine how the investigators interpreted what they found.

The **Discussion** section relates the findings of the investigation back to the hypotheses being tested. Were these confirmed? Disconfirmed? This section also discusses the findings in light of those of other, related studies. A consideration of the implications of the research and future directions for study conclude this section.

The journal article concludes with a list of all the references that were cited in the article.

As you read through the article, ask yourself, "What are the investigators looking for?" "How are they doing this?" "What did they find?" "Is this what they expected to find?" "Why are these findings important?"

Finally, you may find that reading Chapter 13 of the textbook will help you understand published research articles better.

Good luck!

ETHICAL GUIDELINES FOR MAKING OBSERVATIONS

Most disciplines have established a set of ethical guidelines to be used when conducting research with human subjects. The guidelines presented here are those of the American Psychological Association (1982. *Ethical principles in the conduct of research with human participants.* Washington, DC: Author).

The overriding consideration of these guidelines stresses a concern for the **"dignity and welfare"** of the individuals who participate in research. In keeping with this concern, investigators **inform** participants of any aspect of the research that might affect their willingness to serve as subjects. Participants are also told that participation is **voluntary** and that they are free to leave at any point during the study. Researchers have the responsibility to protect the individuals participating in their research from even **minimal risk** of physical or mental discomfort resulting from their observations. After observations have been made, investigators **debrief** participants, telling them what the research was about. Finally, researchers maintain the **confidentiality** of information obtained from participants.

Source: American Psychological Association. (1982). *Ethical principles in the conduct of research with human participants.* Washington, DC: Author.

WRITING A RESEARCH PAPER

Style requirements for writing research papers vary from one discipline to the next. In general, however, the format is similar, and a published set of guidelines is available in most disciplines. In psychology, these appear in the *Publication Manual* of the American Psychological Association. The format presented here follows the APA style. ••(Footnote to be inserted at bottom of this page. Source: *Publication Manual of the American Psychological Association* (4th ed.). (1994). Washington, DC: Author.)

General Comments on Writing

Before launching into the paper itself, a few general remarks on writing are important. The first of these concerns the importance of acknowledging the work of others. When discussing others' findings, or talking about their ideas, you need to indicate them as a source in your paper. Similarly, if you use someone else's wording, indicate this as a quote by placing quotation marks around it and citing the source from which the quote was drawn. Failure to do so leads the reader to believe these ideas or words are your own when they are not, and constitutes plagiarism.

The second general point concerns the use of sexist language. APA style, as that of many other disciplines, avoids the use of sexist, or male-generic, language. Such language uses terms like "he," "his," "man's," and "mankind" to refer to people in general. It was once thought that these terms were generic (hence the term male "generic" language) and referred impartially to individuals of either sex. Research consistently finds that they are not generic and that, quite to the contrary, they promote thoughts about males rather than individuals of either sex. To avoid such terms, one can use the plural, referring to individuals as "they" instead of using sex-specific pronouns such as "he" or "she." The *Publication Manual* contains other suggestions for ways to avoid sexist language.

A last general point concerns the importance of expressing your ideas clearly. Perhaps the most important step in writing clearly is to present your ideas logically. This is most easily done if you outline your ideas before you begin writing. Then you can check the outline for the logical order in which ideas are structured. It is also helpful to write the paper a day or two in advance and then put it aside before you reread it. Doing so allows you to read it with a fresh perspective, catch inconsistencies, and change awkward wording that you might miss otherwise. A clear writing style is also important in expressing ideas clearly. The *Publication Manual* contains useful stylistic suggestions.

Finally, your paper should be typed and *double-spaced throughout.*

Writing the Paper

A research paper includes five main sections: Abstract, Introduction, Method, Results, and Discussion. It also includes a title page and a list of references.

Title page. The title page is a separate page giving the title of the report and, beneath this, a byline indicating the author and the university or agency with which the author is affiliated. Titles should be both brief and informative. The most informative titles mention the variables being investigated. Examples are "The development of empathy in females and males . . ." or "Autonomy in adolescents from single-parent and intact homes . . . ." Typing requirements concerning this and other sections of a research paper are given in the *Publication Manual.*

Abstract. The Abstract summarizes the entire article. In this section, you state the problem you investigated, describe the procedure you used, summarize your results, and state the conclusions you reached. The Abstract is limited to 150 words and appears by itself as the second page of the report. Type and center the word "Abstract" at the top of the page, two spaces above the paragraph.

Introduction. This section begins on the third page immediately below the title of the article, which is centered at the top of the page. Begin the Introduction with a brief summary of the problem you are studying; you can usually state this in two or three sentences. The bulk of the Introduction is devoted to a review of past research and theory as this relates to the variables in your research. The Introduction concludes by stating the relationships— or more specifically, hypotheses—that you expect to find.

Method. The Method section continues on the same page as the Introduction. In this section you describe what you did in carrying out the research: the subjects you used, the materials or conditions you gave them, and the procedure you followed. You should include enough information about each of these so that someone else could conduct essentially the same study simply by reading this section. Type the word "Method" centered on the page and begin the section two spaces below the heading.

Results. This section continues on the same page as the one on which you ended the last section. In the Results section, you summarize differences between the groups or conditions that you studied and indicate whether these are statistically significant. Begin by presenting group means, and then report the results of tests of significance. If you included specific predictions or hypotheses in your Introduction, you should relate the results of the statistical tests to these, indicating in the order in which they were mentioned whether they were confirmed or disconfirmed.

When only two or three conditions are involved, you can give the group means and the results of tests of significance in sentence form. Here is an example of this style:

> The mean empathy scores for the single-parent and intact family groups were 5.36 and 4.98, respectively. This difference was not significant, $t(48) = 1.36$, $p > .05$.

When more groups are involved, it is often helpful to present the data in table form and use figures to display differences and trends.

Discussion. The Discussion follows on the same page as the Results. Begin by relating what you found to what you said you expected to find in the Introduction. Do the findings support your hypotheses? How, if they do, do they extend our knowledge in this area? What implications does this research have for further research in the area? If your hypotheses were not confirmed, you can discuss possible reasons for this outcome. Type the word "Discussion" centered on the page and begin the Discussion section two spaces beneath the heading.

References. An alphabetical listing of references begins on the next page. This list must contain all articles and books referred to in the paper. Also, it should *not* contain any sources that were not referenced in the report. The *Publication Manual* gives the precise forms in which references of different types are to be given.

Source: American Psychological Association. (1993). *Publication Manual of the American Psychological Association* (4th ed.). Washington, DC: Author.

TRANSPARENCY MASTERS

Chapter 1

1. Population Pyramids for the Years 1982, 2000, 2030, and 2080 (Figure 1.1)
2. Changing Ethnic Composition in the United States from 1980 to 1990
3. Gender-Biased Language
4. Developmental Tasks: Infancy and Early Childhood
5. Developmental Tasks: Middle Childhood
6. Developmental Tasks: Adolescence
7. Developmental Tasks: Early Adulthood
8. Developmental Tasks: Middle Age
9. Developmental Tasks: Later Maturity (see Table 1.1)

Chapter 2

10. Characteristics of a Good Theory
11. Comparison of Developmental Models
12. Erikson's Developmental Stages
13. Gilligan's Analysis of Gender Differences

Chapter 3

14. Effects of Hormones on Physical Development and Sexual Maturation at Puberty (Figure 3.3)
15. Sequence of Changes at Puberty
16. Percentage of High School Students Who Have Had Sexual Intercourse: Gender
17. Percentage of High School Students Who Have Had Sexual Intercourse: Grade
18. Percentage of High School Students Who Have Had Sexual Intercourse: Ethnicity (see Table 3.3)
19. Percentage of Others Believed to Be Sexually Active as a Function of Personal Sexual Activity
20. Decision Making About Pregnancy Resolution
21. Eating Disorders

Chapter 4

22. Piaget's Four Stages of Cognitive Development
23. Percentage of Individuals at Different Points from the Mean IQ of 100
24. Sternberg's Components of Intellectual Functioning (Figure 4.10)
25. Gardner's Seven Forms of Intelligence

Chapter 5

26. Family Stress and Family Satisfaction

27. Marriage and Divorce Statistics

28. Communication Patterns That Foster Individuation: Individuality

29. Communication Patterns That Foster Individuation: Connectedness (see Box 5.4)

30. Frequencies of Conflicts Between Adolescents and Parents

31. Parenting Styles and Social Competence

Chapter 6

32. Percentage of Time Spent with Friends, Family, Classmates, or Alone

33. How Adolescents Spend Their Time

34. Stages in the Development of Adolescent Cliques and Crowds

35. Physical Features Noticed When Meeting a Person of the Other Sex

Chapter 7

36. Increase in High School Graduates Over the Past 100 Years (Figure 7.1)

37. Teachers' Ratings of Top Disciplinary Problems—Then and Now (Table 7.1)

38. Percentage of Adolescents Experiencing Violence at School: 8th Grade

39. Percentage of Adolescents Experiencing Violence at School: 10th Grade (see Table 7.2)

40. Characteristics of Gifted Students

Chapter 8

41. Marcia's Four Identity Statuses (Figure 8.1)

42. Ego Identity and Adjustment Measures for Stages of Ethnic Identity

43. Josselson's Dimensions of Relatedness and Their Pathological Poles (Table 8.3)

44. Intimacy Statuses in Adolescence

Chapter 9

45. Relationship Between Dating Stage and Sexual Behaviors

46. Date Rape

47. Kinsey's Continuum of Sexual Orientation (Figure 9.2)

48. Types of STDs

49. Rates of Infection for Men and Women After a Single Act of Intercourse with an Infected Partner

50. Distribution of AIDS Among Adolescents and Young Adults Ages 13–24 (Through June 1993)

51. Leading Causes of Death Among Males (Top) and Females (Bottom) 25–44 Years of Age—United States, 1980–1989 (Figure 9.6)

52. The Progressive Course of HIV Infection

Chapter 10

53. Unemployment Among White and Minority Youth (Figure 10.1)

54. How High School Seniors Spend Their Money (Figure 10.2)

55. Occupations and Median Weekly Earnings of Males and Females, 1992 (Table 10.2)

56. Expert Knowledge

57. Characteristics of Creative Adolescents

58. Perry's Progressions in College Students' Thinking

Chapter 11

59. Values of Adolescents (Figure 11.1)

60. Percent of High School Seniors Indicating That They Agree with Their Parents on Selected Topics: 1975 and 1991 (Figure 11.2)

61. Religious Practices and Beliefs Among High School Seniors: 1976 to 1991 (Table 11.1)

62. Positive Outcomes of Grief

Chapter 12

63. Long-Term Physical Consequences of Childhood Abuse (Physical, Emotional, and/or Sexual)

64. Percentage of High School Seniors Reporting Ever Having Used Drugs (Figure 12.2)

65. Adolescents' Attitudes Toward Drug Use

66. Percentages of Female and Male High School Students Reporting Suicidal Thoughts and Behavior

67. Strategies Used in Coping with Stress

Chapter 13

68. Types of Relationships Found in Research

69. A Sequential Design

BIBLIOGRAPHY OF BOOKS AND ARTICLES

Books

Bandura, A. (1986). *Social foundations of thought and action: A social cognitive theory.* Englewood Cliffs, NJ: Prentice-Hall.

Basseches, M. (1984). *Dialectical thinking and adult development.* Norwood, NJ: Ablex.

Baumrind, D. (1975). Early socialization and adolescent competence. In S. E. Dragastin & G. E. Elder (Eds.), *Adolescence in the life cycle.* New York: Hemisphere Publishing.

Belenky, M. F., Clinchy, B. M., Goldberger, N. R., & Tarule, J. M. (1986). *Women's ways of knowing.* New York: Basic Books.

Blos, P. (1979). *The adolescent passage.* New York: International Universities Press.

Chodorow, N. (1978). *The reproduction of mothering.* Berkeley: University of California Press.

Coles, R. (1970). *Erik Erikson: The growth of his work.* Boston: Little, Brown and Co.

Csikskzentmihalyi, M., & Larson, R. (1984). *Being adolescent.* New York: Basic Books.

Douvan, E., & Adelson, J. (1966). *The adolescent experience.* New York: Wiley.

Elkind, D. (1984). *All grown up and no place to go: Teenagers in crisis.* Reading, MA: Addison-Wesley.

Elkind, D. (1988). *The hurried child: Growing up too fast too soon.* Reading, MA: Addison-Wesley.

Erikson, E. (1963). *Childhood and society.* New York: Norton.

Erikson, E. (1968). *Identity: Youth and crisis.* New York: Norton.

Finkelhor, D., Gelles, R. J., Hotaling, G. T., & Strauss, M. A. (Eds.). (1983). *The dark side of families: Current family violence research.* New York: Sage.

Fowler, J. W. (1981). *Stages of faith: The psychology of human development and the quest for meaning.* San Francisco: Harper & Row.

Freud, A. (1969). Adolescence as a developmental disturbance. In G. Caplan & S. Lebovici (Eds.), *Adolescence,* New York: Basic Books.

Freud, S. (1954). *Collected works, standard edition.* London: Hogarth Press.

Gardner, H. (1983). *Frames of mind.* New York: Basic Books.

Gilligan, C. (1982). *In a different voice: Psychological theory and women's development.* Cambridge, MA: Harvard University Press.

Gilligan, C., Ward, J. V., Taylor, J. M., & Bardage, B. (Eds.). (1988). *Mapping the moral domain.* Cambridge, MA: Harvard University Press.

Gilligan, C., Lyons, N. P., & Hanmer, T. J. (Eds.). (1989). *Making connections.* Troy, NY: Emma Willard School.

Grotevant, H. D., & Cooper, C. R. (Eds.). (1983). *Adolescent development in the family.* San Francisco: Jossey-Bass.

Harris, L. (1988). *Public attitudes toward teenage pregnancy, sex education, and birth control.* New York: Planned Parenthood of America.

Josselson, R. (1987). *Finding herself: Pathways to identity development in women.* San Francisco: Jossey-Bass.

Josselson, R. (1992). *The space between us.* San Francisco: Jossey-Bass.

Lips, H. M. (1993). *Sex and gender: An introduction.* (2nd. ed.). Mountain View, CA: Mayfield.

Loevinger, J. (1976). *Ego development.* San Francisco: Jossey-Bass.

Perry, W. G. (1970). *Forms of intellectual and ethical development in the college years.* New York: Holt, Rinehart & Winston.

Piaget, J. (1952). *The origins of intelligence in children.* New York: International Universities Press.

Piaget, J. (1954). *The construction of reality in the child.* New York: Basic Books.

Rotheram, M. & Phinney, J., (Eds.). (1987). *Children's ethnic socialization: Pluralism and development.* Beverly Hills: Sage Publications.

Selye, H. (1956). *The stress of life.* New York: McGraw-Hill.

Sternberg, R. J. (1985). *Beyond I.Q.: A triarchic theory of human intelligence.* New York: Cambridge University Press.

Strong, B., and DeVault, C. (1994). *Human sexuality.* Mountain View, CA: Mayfield.

Youniss, J., & Smoller, J. (1985). *Adolescent relations with mothers, fathers, and friends.* Chicago: University of Chicago Press.

Youth Indicators. (1993). *Trends in the well-being of American youth.* Washington, DC: U.S. Government Printing Office.

Articles

Bakan, D. (1971). Adolescence in America: From idea to social fact. *Daedalus, 100,* 979–995.

Banks, C. A. McGee. (1993). Restructuring schools for equity: What we have learned in two decades. *Phi Delta Kappa, 75,* 22–28.

Betencourt, H., and Lopez, S. R. (1993). The study of culture, ethnicity, and race in American psychology. *American Psychologist, 4,* 629–637.

Boyes, M. C., and Chandler, M. (1992). Cognitive development, epistemic doubt, and identity formation in adolescence. *Journal of Youth and Adolescence, 21,* 277–304.

Comer, J. P. (1988). Educating poor minority children. *Scientific American, 259,* 42–48.

Finkelhor, D. (1993). Epidemiological factors in the clinical identification of child sexual abuse. *Child Abuse and Neglect, 17,* 67–70.

Gilligan, C. (1984). The conquistador and the dark continent: Reflections on the psychology of love. *Daedalus, 113,* 75–95.

Hartup, W. W. (1993). Adolescents and their friends. In B. Laursen (Ed.), *New directions for child development.* San Francisco: Jossey-Bass.

Hetherington, E. M. (1989). Coping with family transitions: Winners, losers, and survivors. *Child Development, 60,* 1–4.

Labouvie-Vief, G. (1980). Beyond formal operations: Uses and limits of pure logic in life span development. *Human Development, 3,* 141–161.

Newman, J. (1985). Adolescents: Why they can be so obnoxious. *Adolescence, 22,* 635–645.

Nolin, M. J., and Petersen, K. K. (1992). Gender differences in parent-child communication about sexuality. *Journal of Adolescent Research, 7,* 59–79.

Ogbu, J. U. (1992). Understanding cultural diversity and learning. *Educational Researcher, 21,* 5–14.

Phinney, J. (1990). Ethnic identity in adolescents and adults: Review of research. *Psychological Bulletin, 108,* 499–514.

HANDBOOKS AND ACADEMIC JOURNALS

Handbooks

Advances in Adolescent Development
Advances in Developmental Psychology
Annual Review of Psychology
Encyclopedia of Adolescence
Handbook of Adolescent Psychology
Handbook of Developmental Psychology
Life-Span Development and Behavior
New Directions for Child Development

Journals

Adolescence
American Education Research Journal
American Psychologist
Child Abuse and Neglect
Child Development
Cognition
Cognitive Development
Developmental Psychology
Developmental Review
Family Relations
Genetic Psychology Monographs
Gifted Child Quarterly
Harvard Educational Review
Human Development
International Journal of Psychology
Journal of Abnormal Child Psychology
Journal of Abnormal Psychology
Journal of Adolescence
Journal of Adolescent Research
Journal of Applied Developmental Psychology
Journal of Consulting and Clinical Psychology
Journal of Early Adolescence
Journal of Educational Psychology
Journal of Learning Disabilities
Journal of Marriage and the Family
Journal of Research on Adolescence
Journal of Personality and Social Psychology

Journal of Sex Roles
Journal of Youth and Adolescence
Merrill-Palmer Quarterly
Monographs of the Society for Research in Child Development
Morbidity and Mortality Weekly Reports
Psychological Bulletin
Psychological Review
Science

BIBLIOGRAPHY: ETHNICITY AND GENDER

Ethnicity

Banks, C. A. McGee. (1993). Restructuring schools for equity: What we have learned in two decades. *Phi Delta Kappan, 75,* 22–28.

Betancourt, H., & Lopez, S. R. (1993). The study of culture, ethnicity, and race in American psychology. *American Psychologist, 4,* 629–637.

Comer, J. P. (1988). Educating poor minority children. *Scientific American, 259,* 42–48.

Jiobu, R. M. (1988). *Ethnicity and assimilation.* Albany: State University of New York Press.

Ogbu, J. U. (1992). Understanding cultural diversity and learning. *Educational Researcher, 21,* 5–14.

Phinney, J. S. (1990). Ethnic identity in adolescents and adults: Review of research. *Psychological Bulletin, 108,* 499–514.

Phinney, J. S., & Rosenthal, D. A. (1992). Ethnic identity in adolescence: Process, context, and outcome. In G. R. Adams, T. P. Gullotta, & R. Montemayor (Eds.). *Adolescent identity formation.* Newbury Park, CA: Sage Publications.

Phinney, J. S., & Rotheram, M. J. (1987). Children's ethnic socialization: Themes and implications. In M. J. Rotheram & J. S. Phinney (Eds.), *Children's ethnic socialization: Pluralism and development.* Beverly Hills: Sage Publications.

Rosenthal, D. A. (1987). Ethnic identity development in adolescents. In M. J. Rotheram & J. S. Phinney (Eds.), *Children's ethnic socialization: Pluralism and development.* Beverly Hills: Sage Publications.

Rotheram, M. J., & Phinney, J. S. (Eds.). (1987). *Children's ethnic socialization: Pluralism and development.* Beverly Hills: Sage Publications.

Simpson, G. E., & Yinger, J. M. (1985). *Racial and cultural minorities* (5th ed.). New York: Plenum Press.

Spencer, M. B. (1990). Development of minority children: An introduction. *Child Development, 61,* 267–269.

Gender

Belenky, M. F., Clinchy, B. M., Goldberger, N. R., & Tarule, J. M. (1986). *Women's ways of knowing.* New York: Basic Books.

Chodorow, N. (1978). *The reproduction of mothering.* Berkeley: University of California Press.

Gilligan, C. (1982). *In a different voice: Psychological theory and women's development.* Cambridge, MA: Harvard University Press.

Gilligan, C. (1994). The conquistador and the dark continent: Reflections on the psychology of love. *Daedalus, 113,* 75–95.

Gilligan, C., Ward, J. V., Taylor, J. M., & Dardage, B. (Eds.). (1988). *Mapping the moral domain.* Cambridge, MA: Harvard University Press.

Gilligan, C., Lyons, N. P., & Hanmer, T. J. (Eds.). (1989). *Making connections.* Troy, NY: Emma Willard School.

Josselson, R. (1987). *Finding herself: Pathways to identity development in women.* San Francisco: Jossey-Bass.

Josselson, R. (1992). *The space between us.* San Francisco: Jossey-Bass.

Lips, H. M. (1993). *Sex and gender: An introduction* (2nd ed.). Mountain View, CA: Mayfield.

ETHNIC STUDIES INDEXES, JOURNALS, AND PERIODICALS

This list contains the titles of periodicals primarily concerned with the following American ethnic groups:

African Americans

Latinos

Asian Americans

Native Americans

The following periodical indexes are useful:

Chicano Periodical Index

HAPI: Hispanic American Periodicals Index

Index to Periodical Articles by and about Blacks

Sage Race Relations Abstracts

African American Journals and Periodicals

Black Scholar
Ebony
Journal of Black Psychology
Journal of Black Studies
Journal of Negro Education
SAGE: A Scholarly Journal of Black Women
Western Journal of Black Studies

Latino Journals and Periodicals

Aztlan
Bilingual Review, La Revista
El Chicano
Hispanic Journal of Behavioral Sciences
Revista Mujeres

Asian American Journals and Periodicals

Amerasia Journal
Focus on Asian Studies
P/AAMHRC Research Review (Pacific/Asian American Mental Health Research Center)
Vietnam Forum

Native American Journals and Periodicals

Akwesasne Notes

American Indian Culture and Research Journal

American Indian Quarterly

NCAI News (National Congress of American Indians)

News from Native California

Wassaja (national newspaper of Indian America)

General Ethnic Studies Periodicals and Journals

Ethnic Affairs

Ethnic and Racial Studies

Ethnic Forum

Explorations in Ethnic Studies

Immigrants and Minorities

Interracial Books for Children Bulletin

Journal of American Ethnic History

Journal of Ethnic Studies

Race & Class

THE USE OF FILMS IN CLASS

Films and brief clips from movies (videos) can be effective teaching tools, enabling students to relate academic subject matter to their own experiences. In doing so, films transform learning into understanding. The concept of conformity, for instance, is relatively easy to define and lecture on, yet showing a two- to three-minute clip from the film *The Breakfast Club* makes conformity real in a way that few lectures can. In one scene adolescents are shown sneaking out of a detention hall one by one—at the risk of increasing the time they must spend there if caught—to go to a place several of them don't even want to get to. At one point one of the characters verbalizes the absurdity of what he is doing. As viewers, we are witness to the conformity that we have experienced ourselves and seen in others.

When more than a brief clip is shown, it is helpful to use a handout to guide students (see Film Worksheet).

FILM WORKSHEET

Name _____   Class Time _____   Date _____

Name of movie or television program:

Concept being illustrated:

Actions of character(s) and/or situations(s) that illustrate this concept:

A personal experience that illustrates this concept:

NETWORKING: USE OF COMPUTER ON-LINE SERVICES

A new form of electronic discussion group has opened up among scholars, instructors, and researchers. The computer lists appearing below describe several types of electronic groups that are relevant to this course. Most discussion groups are simply that—discussions among those who share an interest in a topic. A few are more scholarly. There is no guarantee of the quality of the lists below. To find out what a list is like, simply try it out. If you have not participated in computer lists before and need assistance, ask the computer consultants at your institution to help you. They will be happy to show you how to get the most out of your system.

Computer Lists

FAMILYSCI is for scholars and educators interested in family relationships and for individuals with an interest in personal relationships. Send subscription request to: LISTSERV@UKCC.UKV.EDU (Internet)

FEMINISM-DIGEST is a digest form of the USENET newsgroup soc.feminism, available on e-mail for those with Usenet. Send subscription request to: FEMINISM-DIGEST@NCAR.UCAR.EDU (Internet), or FEMINISM-DIGEST%NCAR.UCAR.EDU@NCARIO (Bitnet)

You can participate, responding to postings, by sending messages to: FEMINISM@NCAR.UCAR.EDU (Internet), or FEMINISM%NCAR.UCAR.EDU@NCARIO (Bitnet)

H-WOMEN is a list for instructors and scholars in women's history. Send subscription request to: LISTSERV@UICVM (Bitnet), or LISTSERV@UICVM.VIC.EDU (Internet)

WMST-L@UMDD.UMD is a list for scholars in women's studies. Send subscription request to: LISTSERV@UMDD.UMD (Bitnet)

MAIL-MEN is a list in which men and women can discuss men's issues. Send subscription request to: MAIL-MEN-REQUEST@ATTUNIX.ATT.COM (Internet)

INFO-AIDS is a mailing list with information about AIDS. Send subscription request to: info-aids@rainbow.uucp

STOPRAPE is an activist list on sexual assault. Send subscription request to: LISTSERV@BROWNVM (Bitnet), or LISTSERV@BROWNVM.BROWN.EDU (Internet)

TIPS is a list for instructors who "teach in psychology." Send subscription request to: LISTSERV@FRE.FSU.UMD.EDU (Internet), or LISTSERV%FRE.FSU.UMD.EDU@CUNYVM.CUNY.EDU (Bitnet)

How to Subscribe to Lists

Lists with a LISTSERV address are accessed with automated software. To subscribe to the list, type the following message to the list address: SUB<listname><your name>, where <listname> is the name of the list and <your name> is your own name (not your e-mail account id).

Internet addresses, printed immediately beneath the list, are used to subscribe or unsubscribe. Use the form "listname-request account" for administrative questions. Bitnet addresses take the form, "Listname@listhost".

PART II

Approaching Individual Chapters

CHAPTER 1

A Lifespan Perspective on Adolescence

CHAPTER OUTLINE

Adolescents in a Changing Population

The Many Faces of Adolescents

One Face or Two? Sex and Gender Differences
The Colors of Change: Ethnic and Racial Differences
Research Focus/Archival Research: Racial Socialization—Survi*val Tactics in a White Society?*

Defining Adolescence

A Biological Definition
A Psychological Definition
Research Focus/Interviews: A Job? Marriage? Kids? Don't Rush Me—I'm Only 16!
A Sociological Definition

The Lifespan Approach

Lifespan: Change and Continuity
New Ways of Looking at Development
Life Stages Throughout History
    A Time Before Childhood
    The Creation of Adolescence
    A New Age: Youth
    Adulthood in Change
    An Era of Unisex and Uni-Age
Adolescence: A Unique Age

KEY TERMS

Sex Differences	Acculturation	Child Labor Laws
Gender Differences	Cultural Pluralism	Juvenile Justice
Gender Stereotypes	Puberty	Development
Androgynous	Sexual Dimorphism	Growth
Minority	Developmental Tasks	Cohort
Cultural Assimilation	Compulsory Education Laws	Youth

LEARNING OBJECTIVES

After reading the chapter, you should be able to:

1. Define a **model.**

2. Discuss the functions that a **theory** serves.

3. Compare and contrast **nature/nurture, continuity/discontinuity,** and **reductionism/epigenesis.**

4. Summarize the assumptions of: (a) the **environmental model,** (b) the **organismic model,** (c) the **psychodynamic model.**

5. Distinguish **respondent conditioning** from **operant conditioning,** and **positive reinforcement** from **negative reinforcement.**

6. Compare the approaches taken by Havighurst, Skinner, and Bandura, and show how each reflects the environmental model.

7. Discuss **assimilation, accommodation,** and **equilibration.**

8. Summarize the position taken by Gilligan.

9. Discuss the relationship between the **id, ego,** and **superego.**

10. Discuss the similarities and differences in Freud's and Erikson's approaches to personality development.

11. Discuss Chodorow's explanation of gender differences.

CLASS ACTIVITIES

Activity 1-1   Cultural Stereotypes of Adolescents

The portrayal of adolescents in the media frequently reinforces cultural stereotypes. Have students view a television sitcom or movie and identify ways in which adolescents are stereotyped (**Worksheet 1-1**).

Activity 1-2   Interviewing Adolescents

Have students interview several adolescents, preferably differing in age (early vs. late), sex, or ethnicity, so that they can distinguish experiences common to most adolescents from those unique to a particular sex, ethnicity, or stage (early vs. late) in adolescence (**Worksheet 1-2**). Remind them to photocopy the worksheet so that they will have copies for both interviews.

Activity 1-3   Adolescents Today and Yesterday

Have students visit a home for the elderly and get permission to ask several of the residents to describe their adolescence (**Worksheet 1-2**). Alternatively, invite one or more elderly persons as guest speakers to talk to the class about their experiences as adolescents.

Activity 1-4   Generating a Stereotype

Ask students to call out the first word (characteristic) that comes to mind in association with the word "adolescent." Write the terms on the board as the class generates them. Caution the class not to censor themselves by avoiding images that they may regard as insensitive.

WORKSHEET 1-1

Cultural Stereotypes of Adolescents

Name _____ Class Time _____ Date _____

When others react to us as members of a group (defined by age, sex, ethnicity, religion, etc.) rather than as individuals, they are applying a stereotype. How are adolescents stereotyped in the media?

Name of television program or movie:

Central characters and story line:

Portrayal of adolescent character(s):

What stereotype or popular image of adolescents did this show or movie present?

WORKSHEET 1-2

Interviewing Adolescents

Name _____   Class Time _____   Date _____

Record the following information about the person being interviewed:

Age _____   Sex _____   Ethnicity _____

1. What music do you listen to? How important are the lyrics important to you? What are they about? How do they make you feel?

2. How do you spend your free time?

3. When you get together with your friends, what do you do?

4. What qualities do you value most in a friend?

5. What do you like best about yourself? (What would you change if you could?)

6. Have your relationships with your parents changed in the last few years and, if so, how?

7. What do you plan to do when you graduate from high school?

8. How important are your religious and/or political beliefs to you? Have these changed since you were a child?

SUGGESTED READINGS

Ashabranner, B. (1985). *To live in two worlds: American Indian youth today.* New York: Dodd, Mead. Offers a view of the current experiences of American Indian youth.

DuBois, E. C., & Ruiz, Vicki L. (Eds.). (1990). *Unequal sisters: A multicultural reader in U.S. women's history.* New York: Routledge. A collection of readings on the differences and commonalities that divide and unite females in the United States.

Gilmore, D. G. (1990). *Manhood in the making: Cultural concepts of masculinity.* New Haven: Yale University Press. Examines the cultural meaning of "being a man" in different societies.

Howe, I. (1976). *World of our fathers: The journey of the Jews to America and the life they found and made.* New York: Simon and Schuster. Recounts the life of Jews as they came to America.

Kingston, M. H. (1976). *The woman warrior: Memories of a girlhood among ghosts.* New York: Vintage. An account of an Asian American's girlhood.

LeGuin, U. K. (1983). *Left hand of darkness.* A science fiction account of a completely androgynous society, which illuminates the way gender roles permeate current cultures.

Melville, M. B. (Ed.). (1980). *Twice a minority: Mexican-American women.* St. Louis, MO: C.V. Mosby. Presents the problems of minority membership as experienced by many Mexican-American females.

Parks, G. (1991). *Voices in the mirror.* New York, NY: Delacourt. A personal account of growing up black in a white society.

AUDIOVISUALS

1. *Teenagers and Sex Roles.* color / 30 min / sd / VHS. Teenagers struggle with gender issues as they learn what it means to live as an adult in this society. (Soapbox with Tom Cottle series.) University of Wisconsin, 1985.

2. *Adolescence: The Winds of Change.* color / 33 min / optical sound track / VHS. Interviews with adolescents and with the developmentalists John Conger, Jerome Kagan, and David Elkind highlight the biological, sexual, and intellectual changes of adolescence.

3. *Whatever Happened to Childhood?* color / 45 min / film. A look at the pressures experienced by today's children. Kent State, 1983.

4. *A Likely Story Entitled an Invention Called Childhood.* color / 40 min / film. Looks at childhood through history, showing the effects of the Industrial Revolution and examining our present child-centered society. University of Illinois, 1973.

5. Episodes from "Little House on the Prairie" and from "Beverly Hills 90210" or a similar television show. "Little House on the Prairie" is based on Laura Ingalls Wilder's books that portray life over a century ago. "Beverly Hills 90210" is about the experiences of contemporary adolescents.

CHAPTER 2

Theoretical Foundations of Adolescent Development

CHAPTER OUTLINE

Models and Theories

A Model Defined
A Theory Defined
The Environmental Model
The Organismic Model
The Psychodynamic Model

Environmental Theories

Focus on the Biological: Havighurst
Focus on the Personal: Skinner
Focus on the Interpersonal: Bandura

Organismic Theories

Focus on the Biological: Hall
Focus on the Personal: Piaget
Focus on the Interpersonal: Gilligan
*Research Focus/Projective Measures: If Shakespeare Had Been a Woman, Romeo and Juliet Might
Have Survived Romance*

Psychoanalytic Theories

Focus on the Biological: Freud
Focus on the Personal: Horney
Focus on the Interpersonal: Erikson
Focus on the Interpersonal: Chodorow
Research Focus/Erikson's Psychohistorical Approach: A Clinician's Notebook from the Dakota Prairies

KEY TERMS

Model	Conditional Stimulus (CS)	Developmental Task
Theory	Conditional Response (CR)	Observational Learning
Axiom	Operant Conditioning	Reflective Abstraction
Law	Positive Reinforcement	Assimilation
Nature-Nurture Controversy	Negative Reinforcement	Accomodation
Continuity-Discontinuity Issue	Habituation	Equilibration
Reductionism	Stage	Repression
Epigenesis	Libido	Oedipal Complex
Respondent Conditioning	Id	Identity
Unconditional Stimulus (UCS)	Ego	Epigenetic Principle
Unconditional Response (UCR)	Superego	

LEARNING OBJECTIVES

After reading the chapter, you should be able to:

1. Describe recent demographic changes that affect adolescents.

2. Distinguish between **sex differences** and **gender differences.**

3. Distinguish an ethnic group from a **minority** group.

4. Describe **cultural assimilation, acculturation,** and **cultural pluralism.**

5. Summarize the biological changes of **puberty.**

6. Define adolescence from a biological, psychological, and sociological perspective.

7. Explain how **compulsory education law**s, child labor laws, and the **juvenile justice** system contributed to the emergence of adolescence.

8. Understand the lifespan perspective to development.

9. Discuss how our concept of aging has changed throughout history.

10. Discuss parallels between the **developmental tasks** of adolescents, their parents, and their grandparents.

CLASS ACTIVITIES

Activity 2-1   A Theoretical Cocktail Party

Have students break into small groups, each with the name of a theorist such as Skinner, Freud, Erikson, or Chodorow pinned to his or her back and role-play a conversation at a hypothetical cocktail party as to the source of adolescents' problems today.

Activity 2-2   Problem Solving

Use the problems provided on **Worksheet 2-2** (or have the class generate some of their own) and ask students to indicate how each theorist would recommend the problem be treated.

Activity 2-3   Advice Columns

Have students clip problems about adolescents from advice columns (for example, "Dear Abby") and write answers to these working in small groups, each group representing a different theoretical approach (for example, "Dear Siggie," "Dear B. F.," "Dear Erik"). Compare answers in a group discussion involving the entire class.

WORKSHEET 2-2

Problem Solving

Name_____   Class Time_____   Date_____

Indicate below how each theorist would recommend treating these three problems.

	Skinner	Bandura	Freud
Julie's (14) mother recently remarried. Julie is moody and angry, fights with her mother, and has begun to dress and act provocatively.			
Ted's (11) teachers complain that he's disruptive in class, talks out of turn, and doesn't do his classwork.			
Tess (12) and Max (15) continually fight at home. Their parents don't know how to help them get along with each other.			

SUGGESTED READINGS

Chodorow, N. (1989). *Feminism and psychoanalytic theory*. New Haven: Yale University Press. A feminist psychoanalytic perspective on the mother-child relationship.

Erikson, E. H. (1968). *Identity: Youth and crisis*. New York: Norton. Erikson's thoughtful analysis of adolescence.

Freud, S. (1961). Some psychical consequences of the anatomical differences between the sexes. In J. Strachey (Ed.), *Standard edition of the complete psychological works of Sigmund Freud* (Vol. 19). London: Hogarth Press. This essay is central to his theory of psychosexual development, and Freud is also an engaging writer.

Gilligan, C. (1982). *In a different voice*. Cambridge, MA: Harvard University Press. An important statement concerning personality development in females and gender differences in moral thinking.

Tavris, C. (1992). *The mismeasure of woman*. New York: Simon & Schuster. Considers the implications of cultural and scientific assumptions in which the male is taken as the standard against which all are assessed.

Vasta, R. (Ed.). (1989). *Six theories of child development: Revised formulations and current issues*. Greenwich, CT: JAI Press. A current look at developmental theories by experts in the field.

AUDIOVISUALS

1. *Full Circle*. color / 50 min / VHS. An award-winning documentary examining the success of Indians in Washington State in retaining their identity as they live in today's society. Univ. of Calif. Extension Media Center, 1990.

2. *Behavioral Control*. color / 60 min / sd / VHS. Looks at the ethics of behavior modification in situations ranging from subliminal messages affecting us all to its use with hospitalized patients. Hard Choice Series, PBS, 1981.

3. *The Skinner Revolution*. color / 22 min / VHS. A portrait of the man and his ideas and how these have been used to benefit humanity. Univ. of Calif., 1978.

4. *Theory*. color / 20 min / VHS. Examines the role of theory in problem solving in science. Phillips Petroleum Co.

5. *Everybody Rides the Carousel*. color / 73 min / film. Vignettes capture each of Erikson's eight life stages, in two parts. Penn State, 1975.

CHAPTER 3

The Biological Context of Development: Puberty

CHAPTER OUTLINE

The Endocrine System

Hormonal Activity
The Timing of Puberty

The Physical Changes of Puberty

Recollections of an Adolescent Girl
Recollections of an Adolescent Boy
The Growth Spurt
The Reproductive System
Menarche and Spermarche
Research Focus: An Experiment: A Cure for "The Blahs" Before They Begin?
The Secular Trend

The Psychological and Social Implications of Puberty

Two Explanations of the Effects of Physical Change
The Timing of Change: Early and Late Maturers
Research Focus: Longitudinal Design: Body-Image Satisfaction—Mirror, Mirror, on the Wall
Body Image

Eating Disorders

. Dieting
Bulimia and Anorexia
Research Focus: Bias and Blind Controls: Eating Disorders
Obesity

Making Sexual Decisions

Problems Adolescents Face
Sexual Attitudes and Practices

Contraception Use

Lack of Information
Inability to Accept One's Sexuality
Cognitive-Emotional Immaturity

Sex Education: What Adolescents Need to Know

Sources of Information
The Effectiveness of School Programs

KEY TERMS

Endocrine System
Hormones
Androgens
Estrogens
Hypothalamus
Pituitary
Gonads
Primary Sex Characteristics
Secondary Sex Characteristics
Growth Spurt
Fallopian Tubes
Vagina
Clitoris
Glans
Shaft

Prepuce
Epididymis
Vas Deferens
Seminal Vesicles
Prostate Gland
Circumcision
Smegma
Scrotum
Testes
Female Circumcision
Spermarche
Nocturnal Emission
Secular Trend
Asynchrony
Bulimia

Menarche
Uterus
Cervix
Ovaries
Ova (Ovum)
Semen
Sperm
Cowper's Glands
Penis
Urethra
Anorexia
Obesity
Masturbation

LEARNING OBJECTIVES

After reading the chapter, you should be able to:

1. Describe the feedback system regulating the timing of puberty.

2. Distinguish primary and secondary sex characteristics.

3. Summarize the sequence of pubertal development in girls/boys.

4. Discuss the secular trend.

5. Distinguish between direct-effects and mediated-effects models.

6. Define asynchrony.

7. Discuss the effects of early and late maturation for girls/boys.

8. Summarize the distinguishing features of bulimia and anorexia.

9. Define obesity and discuss factors contributing to its occurrence.

10. Discuss the problems adolescents face in making sexual decisions.

11. Summarize adolescent sexual attitudes and practices.

12. Understand the factors contributing to adolescents' use and failure to use contraceptives.

CLASS ACTIVITIES

Activity 3-1   Keeping a Journal

Have students keep a journal as they read this chapter and record memories of their reactions to the physical changes they experienced during puberty. Ask them to indicate the physical changes they liked and those they disliked, and note whether they feel the same about these characteristics today as they did as adolescents (see "Use of Student Journals").

Activity 3-2   Reactions to Menarche/Spermarche

Have students form small, same-sex groups and discuss the feelings they had about menarche/spermarche. Whom did they tell and how did they communicate this? What were the reactions? Had they been adequately prepared for this experience? Would they prepare their children differently?

Activity 3-3   Role-Playing a Parental Discussion About Sex

Ask the class to form small groups in which members role-play a parent and an adolescent having a discussion about sexual behavior, prompted by the parents' belief that the adolescent may be sexually active. Vary the sex of the parent and the sex and the age of the adolescent (for example, a 13- or 17-year-old girl or boy). Does the discussion differ depending on whether it is between a father and son/daughter or mother and son/daughter? Does it differ with the age of the adolescent?

Activity 3-4   Media Portrayal of Adolescent Sexuality

Have students watch a television sitcom with adolescent characters and note how adolescent sexuality is portrayed. Does the portrayal differ from that of adult sexuality? What are the implications of this difference/similarity (use **Worksheet 1-1**).

SUGGESTED READINGS

Brooks-Gunn, J., Boyer, C. B., & Hein, K. (1988). Preventing HIV infection and AIDS in children and adolescents. *American Psychologist, 43,* 958–964. An examination of the risk factors related to HIV infection in adolescents and strategies for preventing transmission of the virus.

Brooks-Gunn, J., & Furstenberg, F. F., Jr. (1989). Adolescent sexual behavior. *American Psychologist, 44,* 249–257. A review of issues and research related to adolescent sexuality.

Gordon, S., & Gilgun, J. F. (1987). Adolescent sexuality. In V. B. Van Hasselt and M. Hersen (Eds.), *Handbook of adolescent psychology.* New York: Pergamon. Discusses sexual decision making and the significance of sexuality to adolescents.

McGuire, P. (1983). *It won't happen to me: Teenagers talk about pregnancy.* New York: Delacorte. Teenagers talk about sex, contraception, and pregnancy.

Morrison, E. (1980). *Growing up sexual: College students' recollections.* New York: Van Nostrand. Personal accounts of sexual experiences and the meaning of one's sexuality.

Sherman, R. T., & Thompson, R. A. (1990). *Bulimia: A guide for family and friends.* New York: Free Press. A well-grounded and practical guide to understanding bulimia.

Voydanoff, P., & Donnelly, B. M. (1990). *Adolescent sexuality and pregnancy.* Newbury Park, CA: Sage. A thorough coverage of teenage pregnancy and related issues.

AUDIOVISUALS

1. *The Human Body: Reproductive System.* color / 16 min / VHS. Animated portrayal of female and male reproductive systems; shows changes occurring in puberty, the functioning of hormones, and fertilization. Kent State University, 1980.

2. *Sexual Development in Children.* color / 45 min / VHS. Considers development through adolescence, exploring cultural norms related to childhood sexuality. Multi-Focus, Inc., 1983.

3. *Sex and Society: Everyday Abuses to Children's Emerging Sexuality.* color / 55 min / VHS. Examines the way societal attitudes can negatively affect the development of sexuality. Adults talk about their negative feelings about their bodies and about sex. Film received honorable mention in the 1991 National Council on Family Relations Media Competition. The Glendon Association, 1991.

4. *Sex Education and AIDS.* color / 30 min / VHS. Presents both sides of the ongoing debate concerning the content of sex education. PBS Video, 1987.

5. *Woman and Man.* color / 52 min / VHS. Considers biological as well as gender differences between females and males. Indiana State University, 1986.

6. *Fear of Fat: Dieting and Eating Disorders.* color / 26 min / VHS. Examines the causes of overeating, anorexia, and bulimia. Penn State, 1987.

CHAPTER 4

Cognitive Development: Processes and Transitions

CHAPTER OUTLINE

How Adolescents Think

Piaget's Stage Theory of Intelligence

A Psychometric Approach to Intelligence

Beyond IQ: Information Processing

Sternberg's Componential Intelligence

Gardner's Seven Facets of the Mind

Thought and the Adolescent

Pseudostupidity
An Imaginary Audience
New Emotions
Arguing
Doubt and Skepticism
Understanding Others

Adolescents in the Classroom

Inductive Reasoning
Deductive Reasoning
Minority Adolescents in the Classroom
Can Adolescents Think Like Scientists?
Study Skills and Knowing What You Don't Know
Metaphors and Meaning: When Is a Ship a State?

KEY TERMS

Sensorimotor Thought	Concrete Operational Thought	Rehearsal
Object Permanence	Mental Operations	Encoding
Schemes	Formal Operational Thought	Metamemory
Assimilation	Intelligence	Pseudostupidity
Accommodation	WAIS-R	Imaginary Audience
Preoperational Thought	Crystallized Intelligence	Personal Fable
Centration	Fluid Intelligence	Social Understanding
Conservation	Sensory Memory	Inductive Reasoning
Reversibility	Short-Term Memory	Deductive Reasoning
Egocentrism	Long-Term Memory	

LEARNING OBJECTIVES

After reading the chapter, you should be able to:

1. Summarize the characteristics of adolescent thought.

2. Describe each of the following: **sensorimotor thought, preoperational thought, concrete operational thought, formal thought.**

3. Discuss **assimilation** and **accommodation.**

4. Define **intelligence.**

5. Describe the **WAIS-R.**

6. Discuss social class, racial, and gender differences in intelligence.

7. Distinguish among **sensory memory, short-term memory,** and **long-term memory.**

8. Discuss Sternberg's approach to intelligence.

9. List Gardner's seven types of intelligence.

10. Describe **pseudostupidity,** the **imaginary audience,** and the **personal fable.**

11. Summarize Selman's stages of **social understanding.**

12. Describe the changes in adolescent thought that allow new forms of learning.

CLASS ACTIVITIES

Activity 4-1   The Development of Humor

Have students get parents' permission to ask an adolescent for the funniest joke(s) he or she knows (using **Worksheet 4-1**). Then have the students read the adolescent's jokes to a child, asking the child why these are funny. Ask students to reach conclusions about the development of humor. The activity can be reversed by asking a child for jokes and reading these to adolescents to determine if the jokes are still seen as humorous.

Activity 4-2   Demonstrating Logical Thinking

The ability to establish truth by testing one idea against another develops in adolescence; prior to this children establish truth by checking their ideas it against things which they can see and touch. Have students get permission from parents to assess which type of proof grade-school children and adolescents use.

WORKSHEET 4-1

The Development of Humor

Name _____ Class Time _____ Date _____

Piaget's stage theory of development describes school children's thought as concrete in comparison to the abstract thought that emerges in adolescence. These differences should be evident in the types of humor children and adolescents enjoy.

Ask an adolescent to tell you the funniest joke(s) he or she knows (remember that you will be repeating these to a child, so caution the adolescent to keep them "clean"). Write the joke(s) in the space below, asking after each, "Why is that funny?" Then tell the joke(s) to a child, asking the same thing. Does the child understand the humor in the joke(s)? Remember to get parental permission before interviewing both the adolescent and the child.

Joke:

"Why is that funny?"

Child's response to the joke when asked, "Why is that funny?"

Does the child understand the humor in the joke? What conclusions can you reach about the development of humor?

58

WORKSHEET 4-2

Demonstrating Logical Thinking

Name _____ Class Time _____ Date_____

You will need poker chips of two colors. Pick up a chip, make a statement about it, and ask your subject if the statement is true. Vary the way you hold up the chips: either visibly or hidden in the hand. Each time you pick up a chip, say "The chip in my hand is either (name one of the two colors) or it isn't." (It isn't necessary to have the color of the chip match the color you mention). Use the worksheet below to record each subject's answers and any remarks. Do the adolescents recognize the logical consistency to the statements; that is, can they answer without seeing the chip? Do the children have to see the chip each time?

Randomly vary the order of these statements from one individual to the next. Tell the subject to indicate whether each statement is true or false. Circle T or F and record any remarks. Be sure to make copies of this form before you begin.

		True	False
1.	(Green chip is visible.) "The chip in my hand is either green or it's not green."	T	F
2.	(Green chip is hidden.) "The chip in my hand is either green or it's not green."	T	F
3.	(Green chip is visible.) "The chip in my hand is either white or it's not white."	T	F
4.	(Green chip is hidden.) "The chip in my hand is either white or it's not white."	T	F
5.	(White chip is visible.) "The chip in my hand is either white or it's not white."	T	F
6.	(White chip is hidden.) "The chip in my hand is either white or it's not white."	T	F
7.	(White chip is visible.) "The chip in my hand is either green or it's not green."	T	F
8.	(White chip is hidden.) "The chip in my hand is either green or it's not green."	T	F

SUGGESTED READINGS

Elkind, D. (1967). Egocentrism in adolescence. *Child Development, 38,* 1025–1034. Elkind's classic paper on the implications of formal thought for adolescents' lives.

Gardner, H. (1983). *Frames of mind.* New York: Basic Books. An alternative approach to intelligence; Gardner presents evidence for seven forms of intelligence, five more than the two measured by most intelligence tests.

Gilovich, T. (1991). *How we know what isn't so: The fallibility of human reason in everyday life.* New York: The Free Press. An interestingly written and up-to-date account of the fallibility of logic in everyday thought.

Ginsburg, H., & Opper, S. (1988). *Piaget's theory of intellectual development* (3rd ed.). Englewood Cliffs, NJ: Prentice-Hall. An easily read and comprehensive presentation of Piaget's theory.

Selman, R. L. (1980). *The growth of interpersonal understanding.* New York: Academic Press. Selman's theory concerning the development of social understanding.

Sternberg, R. J. (1986). *Intelligence applied.* San Diego: Harcourt, Brace, Jovanovich. A view of intelligence that includes practical as well as academic aspects.

AUDIOVISUALS

1. *Memory.* color / 30 min / VHS. Describes sensory, short-term, and long-term memory in a work setting; presents methods for facilitating the organization and retrieval of information. Kent State, 1980.

2. *Adolescence: A Case Study.* color / 20 min / VHS. Explores the psychosocial world of a 17-year-old girl; shows the day to day implications of intellectual development as these take such forms as self-preoccupation and the imaginary audience. CRM Films, 1978.

3. *Intelligence: A Complex Concept.* color / 28 min / VHS. Asks people on the street what intelligence is and explores some of the varied definitions. CRM Films, 1978.

4. *Piaget on Piaget.* color / 45 min / film. Piaget talks about his theory of intellectual development. Yale University, 1978.

5. *Cognitive Development.* color / 18 min / VHS. Looks at Piaget's stage theory and learning theory explanations of cognitive development through each of Piaget's four stages; uses filmed sequences, animation, and special effects. CRM Films, 1973.

CHAPTER 5

Adolescents in the Family

CHAPTER OUTLINE

Changing Relationships with Parents

Turmoil and Change
Calm and Continuity
Change and Continuity
Research Focus: Internal and External Validity: Family Fights

Parents and Adolescents

Styles of Parenting
Research Focus: Direct Observations: Parenting Styles—Like Father, Like Son?
Whose Identity Crisis? Parents and Middle Age
Adolescents' Identity Crisis: Gaining a Sense of Self

Autonomy and Individuation

Autonomy
Individuation: The Developmental Process
Family Interaction and Adolescents' Individuation
The Family Paradigm
Families and Ethnicity
Siblings

Families in Transition

Changing Family Structures
Changing Work Roles: Dual-Earner Families

KEY TERMS

Active Listening	Autonomy
You-Message	Individuation
I-Message	Individuality
Authoritarian Parenting	Connectedness
Authoritative Parenting	Family Paradigm
Permissive Parenting	Problem Analysis
Climacteric	Working Together
Menopause	Role Clarity

LEARNING OBJECTIVES

After reading the chapter, you should be able to:

1. Summarize the nature of changing relationships with parents.

2. Distinguish between **autonomy** and **individuation.**

3. Discuss strategies for better communication.

4. Distinguish **authoritarian parenting, authoritative parenting,** and **permissive parenting.**

5. Discuss the contributions of **individuality** and **connectedness** to individuation.

6. Define **family paradigm.**

7. Summarize differences between Asian American, black, Hispanic, and Native American families.

8. Discuss the contribution of siblings to family life.

9. Discuss the impact of divorce on adolescents and their parents.

10. Summarize the findings related to dual-earner families.

CLASS ACTIVITIES

Activity 5-1   Media Portrayal of Family Conflict

Have students watch a family sitcom and note how conflicts between adolescents and their parents are portrayed. What justifications do adolescents offer for their positions and actions? To what do parents appeal (for example, reason, authority) to get adolescents to comply? (**Worksheet 5-1**)

Activity 5-2   Cultural Stereotypes of Family Roles

Television programs frequently portray family members in stereotyped ways. Have students sample a prime-time network show and record their observations (**Worksheet 5-2**).

Activity 5-3   Role-Playing Active Listening

Have students form dyads in which they role-play active listening between a parent and an adolescent, alternating roles so that each has a turn being the parent and the adolescent.

Activity 5-4   Role-Playing Styles of Parenting

Have students form small groups of three people: a parent, an adolescent, and a neighbor complaining about the adolescent's loud music, driving, or parties. Cycle through three scripts, with students assuming different roles with each portrayal of a different style of parenting.

WORKSHEET 5-1

Media Portrayal of Family Conflict

Name _____   Class Time _____   Date _____

Name of television sitcom:

Nature of family conflict:

Adolescent response(s) to conflict:

Parental response(s) to conflict:

How is conflict resolved:

WORKSHEET 5-2

Cultural Stereotypes of Family Roles

Name _____ Class Time _____ Date_____

SAMPLING A PROGRAM:

    a.   Sample a network by writing the numbers 2, 4, and 7 on three slips of paper and drawing one from a hat.

    b.   After sampling a network, sample a prime-time program (7–10 p.m.) by using the numbers 1–6 to refer to viewing hours, e.g. 1 (8:00–8:30), 2 (8:30–9:00), writing these on six slips of paper, and drawing one from a hat. Continue sampling until you draw a number for a time at which a family sitcom is scheduled.

MAKING OBSERVATIONS:

For each family member, record the following:

	Father	**Mother**	**Sister**	**Brother**
Age (approx.)				
Employment:				
Type of work				
Full-time				
Part-time				
Characterization:				
Independent				
Dependent				
Rational				
Emotional				
Self-reliant				
Yielding				
Willing to take risks				
Sensitive to others' needs				
Makes decisions easily				
Flatterable				

SUGGESTED READINGS

Cooney, P., & Heller, W. (1985). *The teenager's survival guide to moving.* New York: Atheneum. A book for adolescents to help them cope with moving.

Crosby, F. J. (1991). *Juggling: The unexpected advantages of balancing career and home for women and their families.* New York, NY: Free Press. A provocative analysis of the stresses experienced by working women, attributing these to social forces rather than to inherent difficulties in "juggling" career and home. Reviews research showing the advantages to women of working outside the home.

Haley, A. (1976). *Roots: The saga of an American family.* Garden City, NY: Doubleday. A tracing of one African-American family from the days of slave trading to the present.

Hauser, S. T. (1991). *Adolescents and their families: Paths of ego development.* With S. I. Powers and G. G. Noam. New York: The Free Press. Presents intimate portraits of adolescents and their families, and the types of interactions that promote the development of a sense of self.

Kingsolver, B. (1989). *The bean trees.* New York: HarperCollins. Story of a young woman who raises an infant girl "given" to her at a truckstop, and of the meaning of family. HarperCollins.

Noller, P., & Callan, V. J. (1991). *The adolescent in the family.* London: Routledge. Analyzes the contributions of family interactions to adolescent development.

Rofes, E. (Ed.). (1982). *The kids' books of divorce: By and for kids.* Boston: Little, Brown. A compilation of adolescents' reactions to and views on divorce.

Tan, A. (1991). *The kitchen god's wife.* New York: G. P. Putnam. A Chinese mother recounts the amazing events of her life to her daughter.

AUDIOVISUALS

1. *Custody.* color / 94 min / VHS. A dramatic look at the impact of custody battles on family members. Films Incorporated, 1988.

2. *Living with Parents: Conflicts, Comforts, and Insights.* color / 45 min / VHS. Shows adolescents' ambivalence concerning autonomy from parents while desiring to be cared for; discusses communication techniques. Human Relations Media, 1988.

3. *You're Not Listening.* color / 30 min / VHS. Looks at patterns of healthy communication within the family. University of Wisconsin, 1987.

4. *Children and Divorce.* color / 23 min / VHS. A sensitive documentary in which children and adolescents talk about the impact of divorce on their lives, from feelings of sadness and anger to concerns about money and where they will live. NBC and WRC-TV, 1987.

5. *The Child, the Family, and Learning (Bruno Bettelheim).* color / 28 min / VHS. An interview with Bettelheim covers his views on parent and child needs, the extended child dependency period, adolescence and changes in maturity rates, education, and the family. Upon Reflection Series.

CHAPTER 6

Adolescents and Their Friends

CHAPTER OUTLINE

Friendships During Adolescence

Friends and Self-Esteem
Research Focus: Sampling: How Do You Feel at This Moment
Changes in Friendships with Age

Friendship Patterns

What Girls Want in a Friend
What Boys Want in a Friend
Peer Interactions
Interracial Friendships

The Peer Group

Cliques and Crowds
Research Focus: Naturalistic Observation: "Hanging Out"—Cliques and Crowds
Popularity
Dating

Adolescents, Parents, and Peers

Conformity
Values and Peer Pressure
Deviant Behavior and Peer Pressure
The Generation Gap: Is It Widening?

KEY TERMS

Self-disclosure
Enculturation
Clique
Crowd

Social Competence
Conformity
Peer Pressure

LEARNING OBJECTIVES

After reading the chapter, you should be able to:

1. Discuss the functions served by gossip and **self-disclosure** for pre-adolescents and adolescents.

2. Summarize age changes in the friendships of girls and boys.

3. Discuss interracial friendships.

4. Describe the functions of a **clique** and a **crowd.**

5. Know the factors contributing to popularity.

6. Discuss **social competence.**

7. Describe the dating experience.

8. Summarize the factors contributing to conformity.

9. Discuss peer pressure.

10. Discuss factors contributing to the relative influence of parents and peers on adolescent decision making.

CLASS ACTIVITIES

Activity 6-1   Analysis of Popular Music Lyrics

Have students visit a music store and ask what the top-selling tapes/CDs are for (a) early adolescents (11–14) and (b) late adolescents (16–19). Have students listen to the lyrics of each age group's music, noting the differences and the developmental issues these might reflect (**Worksheet 6-1**).

Activity 6-2   Naturalistic Observation: Teen Language

Have students listen to adolescents as they talk to their friends, noting words and expressions not used by adults (for example, parents or teachers) and any other differences distinguishing their speech from that of adults. Ask students to reflect on what functions these might serve for adolescents (**Worksheet 6-2**).

Activity 6-3   High School Crowds

Give students an assignment in which they ask an adolescent to describe the crowds at his or her high school. In class, have students list the crowds that existed in their high schools (**Worksheet 6-3**), comparing these to current crowds. Have the types of crowds changed? Do the same factors contribute to status today?

Activity 6-4   Friendship Survey

Have students break into small groups and survey each other concerning their adolescent friendships (**Worksheet 6-4**).

WORKSHEET 6-1

Analysis of Popular Music Lyrics

Name _____   Class Time _____   Date_____

Top tapes and CDs and themes of lyrics for early adolescents:

Top tapes and CDs and themes of lyrics for late adolescents:

Developmental issues reflected in lyrics:

68

WORKSHEET 6-2

Naturalistic Observation: Teen Language

Name _____ Class Time _____ Date_____

Observe adolescents as they talk to each other and record your observations on this data sheet.

1. Describe the speakers (number, ages, sex, ethnicity, etc.).

2. Note the location in which the conversation takes place (language use can change with different contexts—for example, home, school, etc.).

3. Record the topic(s) of conversation.

4. Note disruptive patterns of speech (for example, choice of words, phrases, patterns of interruption, emotional tone, etc.).

WORKSHEET 6-3

High School Crowds

Name_____ Class Time _____ Date_____

1. Name the crowds that existed in your high school when you were an adolescent (for example, jocks, greasers, populars). Rank these in terms of their status, with 1 being the highest status.

Crowd	Status
_____	_____
_____	_____
_____	_____
_____	_____
_____	_____
_____	_____
_____	_____
_____	_____

2. Ask an adolescent currently in high school to list the crowds in his or her school and rank them for status.

Crowd	Status
_____	_____
_____	_____
_____	_____
_____	_____
_____	_____
_____	_____

WORKSHEET 6-4

Friendship Survey

Name _____ Class Time _____ Date _____

Respondent's Sex: _____ F _____ M

1. How many close friends did you have in early adolescence?

2. How similar in age were they to you?

3. How many of these friends were the same sex as you?

4. How often did you see or talk to these friends?

5. What activities did you and your friends usually engage in when you were together?

6. How important were your friends to you?

     5   4   3   2   1
Not very   Very

7. (Make up several questions of your own.)

SUGGESTED READINGS

Berndt, T. J., & Ladd, G. W. (Eds.). (1989). *Peer relationships in child development*. New York: Wiley. Presents current research on peer relationships in adolescence and childhood.

Dunphy, D. C. (1963). The social structure of urban adolescent peer groups. *Sociometry, 26,* 230–246. Dunphy's classic analysis of the peer group structure in adolescence.

Ephron, D. (1981). *Teenage romance or how to die of embarrassment*. New York: Viking. Written for adolescents, this book discusses first romances.

Hartup, W. W. (1993). Adolescents and their friends. In B. Laursen (Ed.), *New directions for child development*. San Francisco: Jossey-Bass. A scholarly yet readable summary of major issues in adolescent peer relations.

Perry, T. (1984). *Girls, answers to your question about guys*. Los Angeles, CA: Coltrane and Beach. A book designed to help bridge the step to opposite-sex relationships.

AUDIOVISUALS

1. *Psychology of Parenting.* color / 19 min / VHS. Examines the stresses of parenting, presents communication skills for improving relations with adolescents. Films for the Humanities, Inc., 1987.

2. *Children and Stress.* color / 26 min / VHS. Vignettes illustrate common stressful events for children such as competition among peers and low self-esteem. 1985.

3. *The Interpersonal Perception Task.* Looks at nonverbal communication in 30 filmed segments, each followed by an opportunity for the viewer to "decode" the interactions; focuses on themes of intimacy, competition, deception, kinship, and status. University of California Extension Media Center, 1987.

4. *Personality: Adolescence.* color / 21 min / VHS. Explores themes of developing independence, sexual maturation, self-definition and peer support with comments by psychologist Barbara Newman. Kent University, 1978.

CHAPTER 7

Adolescents in the Schools

CHAPTER OUTLINE

Secondary Schools Today

Academic Tracking
School Size
Research Focus: Dependent Variables: Beauty and the Best—Are Looks and Grades Related?
School Climate
Teachers' Attitudes
School Violence
Teaching Peace
Preparing for High School: Junior High or Middle School

Adolescents at School

Literacy, Television, and Homework
Patterns of Achievement
Gender Differences and Achievement
High School Dropouts

Adolescents at the Edge

Gifted Adolescents
Adolescents with Learning Disabilities

Culture and Gender in the Classroom: Education for All

Gender Stereotypes in Teaching Materials
Multicultural Education
Overcoming the Differences

KEY TERMS

Academic Tracking	Jigsaw Classroom
Task Orientation	Microsystem
Performance Orientation	Mesosystem
Gifted	Exosystem
Learning Disability	Macrosystem
Male Generic Language	

74

LEARNING OBJECTIVES

After reading the chapter, you should be able to:

1. Discuss the practice of **academic tracking.**

2. Summarize the attributes of schools contributing to their success.

3. Compare junior high schools with middle schools.

4. Summarize the differences between **task orientation** and **performance orientation** achievement patterns.

5. Discuss the factors related to dropping out in high school.

6. Describe **gifted** adolescents.

7. Discuss **learning disabilities.**

8. Discuss multicultural education.

9. Characterize differences among ethnic groups in terms of four dimensions of personal interaction.

10. Distinguish differences between the **microsystem, mesosystem, exosystem,** and **macrosystem.**

CLASS ACTIVITIES

Activity 7-1   Visiting A High School

Have students visit a high school and get permission to sit in on several classes to identify procedures used to facilitate multicultural education—for example, by presenting material from a multicultural perspective or arranging students in jigsaw classrooms. Have students interview the teachers and ask them what procedures, if any, they use to reach students from different ethnic and racial backgrounds.

Activity 7-2   Survey of Homework and Television

Have several students get permission from a local grade school, junior high, and high school to distribute a survey (**Worksheet 7-2**) during homeroom or a free period concerning the number of hours per week students spend watching television and doing homework. Have students work in small groups collating data for presentation to the class.

WORKSHEET 7-2

Survey of Homework and Television

Name _____   Class Time _____   Date _____

Grade _____

Age _____

Sex _____

1. How many hours a day do you spend watching television?

    1 or less   2–3   3–4   4–5   6 or more

2. How many hours a day do you spend on homework?

    1 or less   2–3   3–4   4–5   6 or more

3. In how many classes do your teachers assign homework four or more times a week?

    1–2   2–3   3–4   4–5   6 or more

4. In how many classes do your teachers assign homework one or two times a week?

    1–2   2–3   3–4   4–5   6 or more

5. In how many classes do your teachers almost never assign homework during the week?

    1–2   2–3   3–4   4–5   6 or more

SUGGESTED READINGS

Fordham, S., & Ogbu, J. U. (1986). Black students' school success: Coping with the "burden of 'acting white.'" *Urban Review, 18,* 176–206. Addresses the problems with achievement that black students face in a white educational system.

Grant, C. (1988). *The world we created at Hamilton High.* Cambridge, MA: Harvard University Press. A study of a high school that met the challenges of racial and ethnic diversity in an urban setting.

Hahn, A. (1987). Reaching out to America's dropouts: What to do? *Phi Delta Kappan, 69,* 256–263. An examination of present policies concerning dropouts.

Kozol, J. (1991). *Savage inequalities: Children in America's schools.* New York: Crown Publishers. A critical analysis of present inequities in the school experiences of adolescents from different racial and economic backgrounds.

LeCompte, M. D., & Dworking, A. G. (1991). *Giving up on school: Student dropouts and teacher burnouts.* Newbury Park, CA: Corwin Press. A compelling analysis of the conditions behind dropping out.

Snow, C. E., Barnes, W. S., Chandler, J., Goodman, I. F., & Hemphill, L. (1991). *Unfulfilled expectations: Home and school influences on literacy.* Cambridge, MA: Harvard University Press. A longitudinal study of the factors contributing to achievement in an ethically diverse group of students.

Foxfire. Illustrates what high school students can learn when given the task of creating a magazine. Penn State, 1973.

AUDIOVISUALS

1. *The School as the Unit of Change.* color / 15 min / VHS. Dr. Goodlad discusses the importance of the school environment for change and envisions the process of change within the metaphor of a garden. Encyclopedia Britannica Educational Corp, 1988.

2. *Specific Learning Disabilities in Adolescence.* color / 33 min / film. Discusses research on learning disabilities in high school students and problems such as dropping out. University of California, 1987.

3. *Cultural Illiteracy.* Narrated by Robert MacNeil and E. D. Hirsch, Jr., this film examines the impact of cultural illiteracy on teenagers' lives and the conditions leading to this, joined by Maya Angelou, Patrick Welsh, and Robert Coles. Festival Films, 1987.

4. *A Gifted Program in Action.* color / 27 min / VHS. Illustrates a model program for gifted students at East School, Terrington, Conn. Encyclopedia Britannica Educational Corp, 1982.

5. *Teaching Is an Attitude.* color / 27 min / VHS. Examines the role of teachers' attitudes as these relate to a variety of issues such as classroom behavior, racial issues, and cooperative learning. Encyclopedia Britannica Educational Corp, 1982.

6. *Dropping Out Equals Broken Dreams.* color / 21 min / VHS. Six adolescents attending an alternative school talk about the conditions that led to their dropping out and what brought them back to school to complete a degree. AIMS Media, 1987.

7. *Dropout.* color / 59 min / VHS. Examines factors related to dropping out and looks at programs that are successful in keeping adolescents in school. Capital Cities Communications, Inc, 1985.

CHAPTER 8

Defining the Self: Identity and Intimacy

CHAPTER OUTLINE

Identity: The Normative Crisis of Adolescence

Identity Defined
The Process of Identity Consolidation

Variations on a Theme of Identity

Identity Statuses
Identity and Personal Expressiveness
Identity Styles
Research Focus: Operationalizing Concepts: You Are How You Think

Identity: Gender and Ethnicity

Gender Differences in Identity Formation
Contributions of Ethnicity to Identity Development

The Self

Self-Concept: Who Am I?
Self-Esteem: Do I Like Myself?

Intimacy: The Self Through Relationships

Intimacy with Oneself
Intimacy with Others
Research Focus: Path Analysis: Too Young for Intimacy?

Intimacy and Identity: Different Paths to Maturity?

Development in Adolescence
Development in Females
Dimensions of Relatedness
Gender Differences in Relatedness
A New Definition of Maturity

KEY TERMS

Identity	Identity-Diffused	Self-Concept
Identification	Personal Expressiveness	Self-Esteem
Identity Formation	Ethnic Identity	Intimacy
Identity-Achieved	Unexamined Ethnic Identity	Agency
Identity-Foreclosed	Ethnic Identity Search	Communion
Moratorium	Achieved Ethnic Identity	

LEARNING OBJECTIVES

After reading the chapter, you should be able to:

1. Understand Erikson's use of the terms identity and crisis.

2. Discuss the process of identity consolidation.

3. Distinguish **identity achievement, identity foreclosure, moratorium,** and **identity diffusion.**

4. Summarize research related to gender.

5. Summarize the contribution of ethnicity to **identity formation.**

6. Discuss **self-concept** and **self-esteem.**

7. Define **intimacy** and summarize its relationship to **identity.**

8. Summarize Josselson's dimensions of relatedness.

9. Distinguish different definitions of maturity.

CLASS ACTIVITIES

Activity 8-1   Role-Playing Identity Statuses

Have students form small groups and role-play adolescents discussing the need to decide their future occupation, with each student role-playing a different identity status.

Activity 8-2   Cultural Images of Ethnicity

Ask students to watch current sitcoms for their portrayal of ethnicity. Are Asian Americans, African Americans, Hispanics, and Native Americans represented? Are they portrayed in ways that differ from each other? From the majority culture (**Worksheet 8-2**)?

Activity 8-3   Small Group Discussions of Self-Concept in Adulthood and Adolescence

Have students form small discussion groups and write on one side of a 3 x 5 index card the characteristics that currently best describe themselves, and on the other side the characteristics that best described them as adolescents. Have each student share these with other members of the group (see "Guidelines for Conducting Group Discussions").

Activity 8-4   Perspectives on Maturity

Have students work in small mixed-sex groups with **Worksheet 8-4,** comparing their answers when all have completed the worksheet.

WORKSHEET 8-2

Cultural Images of Ethnicity

Name _____ Class Time _____ Date _____

For each sitcom, record the number of characters who are:

African   Asian   Native
American   American   American   Caucasian   Hispanic

Which characters have major or minor roles?

Are minority characters portrayed primarily in terms of their ethnicity or their personality (for instance, how well represented are components of their identity such as occupation, marital status, beliefs)?

What do minority/majority characters contribute to the advancement of the plot?

WORKSHEET 8-4

Perspectives on Maturity

Name _____ Class Time _____ Date _____

Does maturity take a different form for females and males? More specifically, do the strengths that comprise maturity differ for females and males? Answer the questions below and then compare your answers with others in your group.

Gender: _____ Female _____ Male

1. What does maturity mean to you?

2. When you think of yourself as a mature person, what qualities come to mind?

3. What qualities do you value most in a person?

SUGGESTED READINGS

Gibbs, J. T., Huang, L. N., & associates. (1989). *Children of color: Psychological interventions with minority youth.* San Francisco: Jossey-Bass. Discusses the development of minority youth and recommends intervention approaches.

Josselson, R. (1988). *The embedded self: I and thou revisited.* In D. K. Lapsley & F. C. Power (Eds.), *Self, ego, and identity: Integrative approaches.* New York: Springer-Verlag. A theoretical review of theory and research as these relate to definitions self and maturity.

Josselson, R. (1992). *The space between us.* San Francisco: Jossey-Bass.

Kingsolver, B. (1990). *Pigs in heaven.* New York: HarperCollins. Story of a Native American girl being raised by a Caucasian single parent, and the interplay of individual and cultural identity.

Loevinger, J. (1990). Ego development in adolescence. In R. E. Muss (Ed.), *Adolescent behavior and society: A book of readings* (4th ed.). San Francisco: McGraw-Hill. A summary of the authors own stages of ego development.

Phinney, J., & Rotherman, M. J. (Eds.). (1987). *Children's ethnic socialization: Pluralism and development.* Newbury Park, CA: Sage. Covers issues of socialization and identity formation.

Power, S. (1994). The grass dancer. New York: G. P. Putnam's Sons. Story of a Native American growing into manhood with the aid of living relatives and ancestral spirits.

Tan, A. (1989). *The joy luck club.* New York: G. P. Putnam. Intertwining stories of Chinese-American mothers and daughters that illustrate generational tensions related to cultural identity. (Also available in video.)

Tanner, D. (1990). *You just don't understand.* New York, NY: Morrow. An insightful analysis of gender differences in approaches to relationships.

AUDIOVISUALS

1. *Self-Esteem: Feeling Good About Yourself.* color / 20 min / VHS. Examines the problem of low self-esteem as this impacts individuals' ability to cope with problems and enjoy life. Sandler Institutional Films, Inc, 1984.

2. *Self Identity/Sex Roles: I Only Want You to Be Happy.* color / 16 min / VHS. Three women illustrate conflicting views concerning the female role; addresses issues of biological differences to gender roles, self-determination, and pressures to conform experienced by either sex. CRM, 1975.

3. *Invisible Walls.* B&W / 12 min / VHS. A close look at personal space recorded by individuals' reactions as this is violated. University of California Extension Media Center, 1969.

CHAPTER 9

The Sexual Self: Close Relationships in Late Adolescence

CHAPTER OUTLINE

KEY TERMS

Gender-Role Stereotypes
Androgynous
Eros
Storge
Ludus
Mania
Pragma

Agape
Double Standard
Heterosexual
Homosexual
Bisexual
Sexually Transmitted Disease (STD)
Chlamydia

Gonorrhea
Genital Warts
Syphilis
Pubic Lice
HIV Infection
AIDS

LEARNING OBJECTIVES

After reading the chapter, you should be able to:

1. Discuss the masculine and feminine sex roles and androgyny.

2. Distinguish different styles of loving.

3. Discuss definitions of sexual orientation.

4. Summarize the biological factors contributing to sexual orientation.

5. Describe the sexual response cycle.

6. Discuss common misconceptions concerning sexual functioning.

7. Describe the factors contributing to adolescents' decisions to abort an unplanned pregnancy or carry the pregnancy to term.

8. Discuss sexually transmitted diseases.

9. Discuss the factors that increase an adolescent's risk of contracting an STD.

10. Summarize the stages of HIV infection and AIDS.

11. Describe what adolescents can do to reduce the risk of infection with a sexually transmitted disease.

CLASS ACTIVITIES

Activity 9-1   Advice Columns on Intimacy

Ask students to clip problems about intimacy from advice columns, putting the problem on one side of an index card and the answer on the other. Have students work in small groups, write answers to problems brought in by other students, then compare their answers to those of the advice columnist.

Activity 9-2   Role-Playing First Moves

Pass out index cards, have students identify themselves only by sex, and ask them to write out the first moves they have used to initiate a sexual encounter: (a) as an adolescent and (b) as an adult. Have students form small mixed-sex groups in which they compare first moves by age (adolescents and adults) and sex (females and males).

Activity 9-3   Debate on School Health Clinics

Invite several members of the class to prepare a panel discussion/debate on school health clinics providing condoms and birth control counseling to students.

Activity 9-4   Guest Speaker on Contraception and STDs

Invite a campus or community health care professional to class to discuss adolescents' use/nonuse of contraceptives and sexually transmitted diseases common among adolescents.

SUGGESTED READINGS

McGuire, P. (1983). *It won't happen to me: Teenagers talk about pregnancy.* New York: Delacorte. Teenagers talk about sex, contraception, and pregnancy.

Morrison, E. (1980). *Growing up sexual: College students' recollections.* New York: Van Nostrand. Personal accounts of sexual experiences and the meaning of one's sexuality.

Tanner, D. (1990). *You just don't understand.* New York: William Morrow. An analysis of gender differences in communication.

Voydanoff, P., & Donnelly, B. M. (1990). *Adolescent sexuality and pregnancy.* Newbury Park, CA: Sage. A thorough coverage of teenage pregnancy and related issues.

AUDIOVISUALS

1. *No Means No: Understanding Acquaintance Rape.* color / 33 min / VHS. Presents a mock trial on date rape and discusses how to know when no means no. Winner of the 1992 National Council on Family Relations Media Competition. Human Relations Media, 1992.

2. *What If I'm Gay?* color / 30 min / VHS. Questions posed by a teenager after discovering he is gay. Received honorable mention in the 1989 National Council on Family Relations Media Competition. Coronet/MTI.

3. *A Million Teenagers.* color / 25 min / VHS. Peer counselors discuss STDs with a class. Winner of 1992 National Council of Family Relations Media Competition. Churchill Media.

4. *No Rewind: Teenagers Speak Out on HIV and AIDS Awareness.* color / 22 min / VHS. HIV positive adolescents talk to their peers. ETR Associates.

5. *Project Future: Teenage Pregnancy, Childbirth, and Parenting.* color / 145 min / VHS. Follows prospective teen parents through pregnancy to three months following birth. Winner of 1992 National Council on Family Relations Media Competition. Vida Health Communications.

6. *Teen Issues: Date Rape.* color / 27 min / VHS. Defines date rape and examines societal attitudes contributing to this problem; discusses precautions and ways to cope with personal trauma. Indiana University, 1987.

7. *And Baby Makes Two.* color / 25 min / VHS. Looks at the difficulties teenage mothers face and at programs designed to help. Syracuse University, 1988.

CHAPTER 10

Careers and College

CHAPTER OUTLINE

Adolescents at Work

Part-Time Employment
Dropouts and Employment

Choosing a Vocation

Social-Cognitive Theory
Ginzburg: Vocational Stages
Super: Careers and the Self-Concept
Holland: Personality Types and Work

Joining the Workforce

Job Availability
Women and Work
Minorities and Work

Intervention Programs: Strategies for Change

Counselors as Change Agents
Research Focus: Quasi-Experimental Designs: Precollege Programs for Minority Youth
Irrational Beliefs and Maladaptive Myths

Adolescents and College: Thinking About Ideas

New Solutions to Old Problems: Structural Analytical Thinking
Research Focus: Factorial Designs: Career Indecision—Don't Push Me; I'm Still Thinking
How College Changes the Way Adolescents Think
Gender Differences in Intellectual Development
Research Focus: Theory-Guided Research: How Sexist Is Our Language?

Adolescents as Experts

Experts and Novices
Knowledge of One's Culture: Everybody's an Expert

Putting Knowledge to Work

Active Knowledge
Inert Knowledge
Thinking as Problem Solving

Creativity

Characteristics of Creativity
Origins of Creativity in Adolescents

Adolescent Decision Making

Personal Effectiveness
Dealing with Everyday Problems

KEY TERMS

Fantasy Stage	Investigative Personality Types	Dialectical Reasoning
Tentative Stage	Artistic Personality Types	Dualistic Thinking
Realistic Stage	Social Personality Types	Relativistic Thinking
Growth Stage	Enterprising Personality Types	Commitment in Relativism
Exploration Stage	Conventional Personality Types	Subjective Knowledge
Establishment Stage	Inductive Reasoning	Procedural Knowledge
Maintenance Stage	Deductive Reasoning	Constructive Knowledge
Decline Stage	Structural Analytical Thinking	Inert Knowledge
Realistic Personality Types	Propositional Reasoning	IDEAL

LEARNING OBJECTIVES

After reading the chapter, you should be able to:

1. Discuss part-time employment and spending patterns among adolescents.

2. Use a social-cognitive framework to explain vocational choice.

3. Summarize Ginzburg's vocational stages.

4. Explain Super's theory of occupational choice.

5. Distinguish Holland's six personality types.

6. Discuss the vocational aspirations of and difficulties facing females entering the workforce.

7. Describe the problems facing minority youth who are preparing to enter the workforce and the types of intervention that are needed.

8. Relate **structural analytical thinking, formal thinking, dialectical reasoning,** and **propositional reasoning.**

9. Summarize the progression from **dualistic thinking,** to **relativistic thinking,** to **commitment in relativism.**

10. Discuss differences between **subjective knowledge, procedural knowledge,** and **constructive knowledge.**

11. Summarizes differences in thinking between experts and novices.

12. Discuss cultural knowledge as a form of expertise.

13. Explain **inert knowledge.**

14. Discuss creativity.

CLASS ACTIVITIES

Activity 10-1   Vocational Goals

Have students discuss their vocational goals in small groups. Ask them to consider similarities and differences between their goals and those of their parents; what factors were influential in their decisions about a vocation; and the most important advice they could give someone who is deciding on a vocation.

Activity 10-2   Part-Time Employment

Have students interview one or more adolescents (obtaining parental permission) who hold part-time jobs (**Worksheet 10-2**).

Activity 10-3   Expert Knowledge

Have students break into small groups and form pairs in which each partner identifies an area of his or her expertise and agrees to bring to class a short newspaper or magazine article on the *other's* area of expert knowledge. In the following class meeting, have the class break into groups again. Have students read the article on which they have expert knowledge and a second article, brought in for someone else, for which they do not have expert knowledge. Have students summarize each article from memory. Then have students compare their expert and non-expert summaries.

Activity 10-4   Structural Analytical Thinking

Have students form small discussion groups (see "Guidelines for Conducting Group Discussions") in which each introduces a personal problem such as that experienced by Connie and Janice in the chapter and describes her or his attempts at a solution. Have students analyze these in terms of formal versus structural analytical thinking. In the case of the former, have them generate approaches based on structural analytical thinking that might offer new possibilities of success.

WORKSHEET 10-2

Part-Time Employment

Name_____ Class Time _____ Date_____

Subject's Age _____ Sex _____

1. How long have you worked at this part-time job? [1]

2. In your opinion, what are the major advantages of working part-time?

3. In your opinion, what are the major disadvantages of working part-time?

4. What experience does this job give that you can transfer to the work that you eventually plan to do?

5. If you did not need the money, would you still work part-time? Why or why not?

_____

[1] "Prompt" with "I see," "uh-huh," and "Tell me more about that."

SUGGESTED READINGS

Baron, J., & Brown, R. V. (Eds.). (1991). *Teaching decision-making to adolescents.* Hillsdale, NJ: Erlbaum. A practical guide to decision-making skills for adolescents.

Belenky, M. F., Clinchy, B. M., Goldberger, N. R., & Tarule, J. M. (1986). *Women's ways of knowing: The development of self, voice and mind.* New York: Basic Books. An analysis of the approaches women take to truth and knowledge and how these relate to and reflect the development of the self.

Career Development Quarterly. A journal publishing research on career development, including research on gender and minority issues.

Chi, M. T. H. (1985). Interactive roles of knowledge and strategies in the development of organized sorting and recall. In S. F. Chipman, J. W. Segal, & R. Glaser (Eds.), *Thinking and learning skills,* Vol. 2. Hillsdale, NJ: Erlbaum. Discusses research on expert knowledge and the ways this influences thinking and recall.

Cole, S. (Ed.). (1980). *Working kids on working.* New York: Lothrop, Lee & Shepard. Adolescents discuss their own experiences of working.

Faludi, S. (1991). *Backlash: The undeclared war against American women.* Crown Publishers. A provocative analysis of backlash, ranging from media images of burned-out career women to subtle messages threatening loss of love, that has followed the winning of new rights by American women.

Lips, H. M. (1991). *Women, men, and power.* Mountain View, CA: Mayfield Publishing Company. A current, research-based analysis of gender and power, with a chapter on power in the workplace.

Perry, W. G. (1970). *Forms of intellectual and ethical development in the college years.* San Francisco: Holt, Rinehart, & Winston. An analysis of the approaches college men take to truth and knowledge and how these relate to and reflect the development of the self.

Schulman, M. (1991). *The passionate mind: Bringing up an intelligent and creative child.* New York, NY: Free Press. A discussion of conditions in the home and classroom that foster creativity.

AUDIOVISUALS

1. *The New Pacific: Education.* color / 50 min / VHS. Examines the relationship between education and cultural attitudes in the U.S., Japan, Korea, and Samoa. University of California, 1988.

2. *A+ Student: How to Study and Take Notes.* color / 22 min / film. Looks at two study programs; includes scanning, self-questioning, self-testing, and note-taking. Syracuse University, 1987.

3. *Classroom Management: The Student's Role.* color / 27 min / VHS. Demonstrates the importance of relating classroom learning to experiences outside the classroom. Encyclopedia Britannica Educational Corp., 1982.

4. *Children of the Tribe.* color / 27 min / film. Looks at education from childhood to college years in Japan, comparing cultural approaches to child rearing and education in Japan and in the West. Kent State, 1980.

5. *Careers in Mathematics: A Different View.* color / 19 min / VHS. Shows young men and women at work in different careers; in interviews they talk about the math and science skills needed for their type of work. Disney, 1986.

6. *The Money Tree.* color / 21 min / VHS. Attempts to give students insight into the difficulties brought about by monetary problems. AIMS Media, 1983.

CHAPTER 11

Facing the Future: Values in Transition

CHAPTER OUTLINE

The Values of Adolescents
Values and Identity
A Developing Morality

Social-Cognitive Theory and Moral Development
Internalizing Standards
Considering Intentions
Questioning Values
Acting Morally
Critique of Social-Cognitive Theory

Kohlberg and Moral Development: Morality as Justice
Preconventional Moral Reasoning
Conventional Moral Reasoning: Internalizing Standards
Postconventional Moral Reasoning: Questioning Values
Research Focus: Surveys: Death of a High School Basketball Star
Critique of Kohlberg's Theory

Gilligan: An Ethic of Care
Level 1: Caring for Self (Survival)
Transition: From Selfishness to Responsibility
Level 2: Caring for Others (Goodness)
Transition: From Conformity to Choice
Level 3: Caring for Self and Others (Truth)
Critique of Gilligan's Theory
Comparison of Gilligan's and Kohlberg's Approaches

Freud: Morality and the Superego
Critique of Freud's Theory

Adolescents' Religious Beliefs
Importance of Religion
Research Focus: Within-Subjects Design: Forgiveness

KEY TERMS

Preconventional Moral Reasoning   Superego
Conventional Moral Reasoning   Conscience
Postconventional Moral Reasoning   Identification
Ethic of Care

LEARNING OBJECTIVES

After reading the chapter, you should be able to:

1. Summarize the relationship between values and identity statuses.

2. Discuss moral development from a social-cognitive perspective.

3. Distinguish **preconventional moral reasoning, conventional moral reasoning,** and **postconventional moral reasoning.**

4. Summarize the way females resolve conflict at each level in Gilligan's **ethic of care.**

5. Compare Gilligan's and Kohlberg's approaches.

6. Describe Freud's explanation of moral development.

7. Critique Freud's theory of moral development.

8. Discuss adolescents' religious beliefs.

CLASS ACTIVITIES

Activity 11-1   Discussing Religious Stereotypes

Read (assign) one of Garrison Keillor's short stories in class about life in Lake Woebegon (or play one of his tapes) in which he describes the Lutherans and the Catholics. Have the class break into small groups and discuss how Keillor's characterization of the Lutherans and the Catholics is similar (different) to their feelings about their own and others' religions (ways of life).

Activity 11-2   Role-Playing Moral Stances

Have students break into small groups and role-play a moral dilemma (for example, Heinz and the druggist, the moles and the porcupine) with students assuming different levels in Kohlberg's and Gilligan's models.

Activity 11-3   Panel Discussion on Values and Religion

Invite campus religious leaders for a panel discussion on the importance of values and religion in adolescents' lives.

SUGGESTED READINGS

Fowler, J. W. (1981). *Stages of faith: The psychology of human development and the quest for meaning.* San Francisco: Harper & Row. An important work examining the development of a religious identity.

Gilligan, C. (1982). New maps of development: New visions of maturity. *American Journal of Orthopsychiatry, 52,* 199–212. Gilligan contrasts different approaches to moral issues taken by females and males and traces these to alternative modes of self-definition.

Gilligan, C., Ward, J. V., & Taylor, J. M., with Bardige, B. (1988). *Mapping the moral domain.* Cambridge, MA: Harvard University Press. Gilligan and others extend the arguments advanced in *In a Different Voice* to a cross-section of life settings and challenge existing formulations of morality.

Kohlberg, L. (1975). The cognitive-developmental approach to moral education. *Phi Delta Kappan, 56,* 670–677. Kohlberg summarizes his important theory on the development of moral reasoning.

AUDIOVISUALS

1. *Processione: A Sicilian Easter.* color / 28 min / VHS. Looks at the "Procession of the Mysteries," a ritual religious procession, and examines the importance of ritual. University of California Extension Media Center, 1989.

2. *Lying and Cheating.* color / 29 min / VHS. Sixth-graders talk about lying and how it makes them feel. University of Wisconsin, 1985.

3. *Introduction to Moral Development.* color / 29 min / film. Kohlberg on his six stages of moral reasoning. Penn State, 1977.

4. *Teaching Strategies for Moral Development.* color / 29 min / film. Illustrates how knowledge of stages of moral reasoning can help students reason in more sophisticated ways. Penn State, 1977.

5. *Morality: The Process of Moral Development.* color / 28 min / film. Interviews children to young adults concerning moral issues. University of Michigan, 1977.

6. *What's Right For You?* color / 29 min VHS. Helps teenagers explore their values as these relate to sexuality. Candid discussions by boys and girls related to sexual issues. Indiana University, 1976.

CHAPTER 12

Atypical Development in Adolescence

CHAPTER OUTLINE

Stress and Coping

Alienation and the Failure to Cope

Juvenile Delinquency

Adolescents and Drugs

Depression

Suicide

Gender and Ethnic Differences
Warning Signs
Risk Factors
Counseling and Prevention

Schizophrenia

Warning Signs
Distinguishing Features
Prognosis

KEY TERMS

Stress	Cocaine
General Adaptation Syndrome (GAS)	Depressants
Coping	Inhalants
Stress-Inoculation Training	Barbiturates
Attributional Error	Quaaludes
Alienation	Tranquilizers
Juvenile Delinquency	Narcotics
Status Offenses	Hallucinogens
Index Offenses	Anabolic Steroids
Drug Dependence	Affective Disorders
Marijuana	Depression
Stimulants	Schizophrenia
Amphetamine	

LEARNING OBJECTIVES

After reading the chapter, you should be able to:

1. Enumerate common sources of **stress** for adolescents.

2. Discuss how adolescents **cope** with stress.

3. Summarize the components of a **stress-inoculation training** program.

4. Discuss the problems runaway adolescents face.

5. Characterize the patterns of abuse and neglect experienced by adolescents.

6. Discuss sexual abuse.

7. Distinguish between **status offenses** and **index offenses**.

8. Enumerate the factors associated with **juvenile delinquency**.

9. Explain **drug dependence**.

10. Discuss the relationships among adolescents' use of alcohol, cigarettes, and **marijuana**.

11. Distinguish between **stimulants** and **depressants**.

12. Discuss **depression** in adolescence.

13. Know the warning signs of suicide.

14. Define **schizophrenia**.

CLASS ACTIVITIES

Activity 12-1   Survey of Community Support

A.   Have students determine what community agencies and facilities exist to help adolescents who are in need. Are there shelters for runaways staffed by individuals trained to work with adolescents in a crisis situation? Is there a suicide hot line? Are there intervention programs that focus on family violence and abuse? Are there support groups for adolescents and parents with similar problems?

B.   Even with the existence of community agencies, many adolescents remain without help because those they turn to for help are unaware of the programs that exist. Once the class has determined what programs are available for adolescents in need, have them find out whether individuals in the community are knowledgeable about these and could direct an adolescent in need to the appropriate agency; for example, survey teachers in high schools/junior highs, dial Information and ask if there is a number for a suicide hot line, speak with youth directors in churches/synagogues and ask if they know what community support exists and what support they offer adolescents in need.

Activity 12-2   Coping Assertively

Effective coping frequently involves being assertive with others. Assertiveness is saying what one thinks and feels and negotiating positive outcomes in which others as well as oneself benefit; it differs from aggressiveness and passivity. Aggressiveness involves the domination of another without consideration for that person's feelings; it is usually hurtful in some way to the other individual. Passivity involves a denial of one's feelings or needs; it is emotionally dishonest and rarely results in a satisfactory outcome for the individual or those involved with that person. Have the class form small groups and role-play assertive, aggressive, and passive responses to the situations on **Worksheet 12-2**.

WORKSHEET 12-2

Coping Assertively

Name _____   Class Time _____   Date _____

For each of the following situations, role-play one of the following ways of coping (a) assertively, (b) aggressively, and (c) passively.

1. You have been waiting in a long line at the Department of Motor Vehicles. Just as you get to the window, someone asks if they can step in front of you because they are in a rush. You say:

   Assertive

   Aggressive

   Passive

2. Someone who is not a close friend says, "I'm having houseguests this month and don't have enough room to accommodate them all. Since you're going to be out of town when they're here, could I have one of them stay at your house?" You answer:

   Assertive

   Aggressive

   Passive

Sample Responses:

1. *Assertive:* "No, it would not be fair to the people who have been waiting behind me."

   Aggressive: "Back off, you can't cut in line here!"

   Passive: "I dunno, I guess so."

2. *Assertive:* "No, I wouldn't want someone I don't know staying in my home."

   Aggressive: "Are you crazy? That's a nervy request to make!"

   Passive: "Oh, I guess so."

SUGGESTED READINGS

Bronfenbrenner, U. (1986). Alienation and the four worlds of childhood. *Phi Delta Kappan, 67,* 430–436. A compelling analysis of social forces leading to alienation and suggestions for overcoming these.

Cohen, S., & Cohen, C. 1984. *Teenage stress.* New York: Evans and Co. An easily read and practical resource for understanding the stresses adolescents experience.

Gelles, R. J., & Cornell, C. P. (1990). *Intimate violence in families* (2nd ed.). Newbury Park, CA: Sage. An authoritative and easily read overview of current approaches to understanding and treating family violence.

Ianni, A. J. (1989). *The search for structure: A report on American youth today.* New York: The Free Press. An insightful report on current influences in adolescents' lives based on interviews with thousands of teenagers.

Patton, M. Q. (Ed.) (1991). *Family sexual abuse: Frontline research and evaluation.* Newbury Park, CA: Sage. An important review of research on family sexual abuse and intervention programs.

AUDIOVISUALS

1. *Surviving Sexual Abuse.* color / 27 min / VHS. Powerful presentation by two women and two men as they talk about being abused as children and adolescents and how they survived this trauma. University of California Extension Media Center, 1987.

2. *It Shouldn't Hurt to Be a Kid.* color / 57 min / VHS. Examines a system of peer helping; interviews peer helpers and adults. Indiana University, 1987.

3. *Coping with Depression.* color / 20 min / VHS. Looks at the factors contributing to depression and ways of coping with it. Filmfair Communications, 1987.

4. *Teen Suicide: Who, Why, and How You Can Prevent It.* color / 62 min / VHS. Gives an overview of adolescent suicide and examines factors associated with suicide attempts, warning signs, and prevention programs, in 4 parts. Guidance Associates, 1986.

5. *Youth Stress.* color / 24 min / VHS. Looks at the causes and problems associated with stress in adolescents, and suggests ways of coping. Indiana University, 1983.

6. *Four Men Speak Out on Surviving Childhood Sexual Abuse.* color / 30 min / VHS. Survivors of sexual abuse discuss its effects on their lives and how they are recovering from it. Honorable mention at the 1992 National Council on Family Relations Media Competition. Varied Directions International.

7. *The I Can Do That Theater.* color / 62 min / VHS. Documentary of six recovering Asian-American substance abusers at a residential therapeutic facility and the therapeutic effect of theater (contains street language). University of California Extension Media Center, 1990.

8. *Just Beer.* color / 17 min / VHS. Illustrates the physical effects of beer and looks at addiction and its effects in adolescents' lives. Kent State, 1984.

9. *Steroids: Shortcut to Make Believe Muscles.* color / 35 min / VHS. Presents the negative side effects associated with steroid use. International Film Bureau.

10. *Epidemic! Drugs and Alcohol.* color / 27 min / VHS. Looks at the physical, cognitive, and social effects of drug and alcohol abuse and at influences leading to their use. Kent State, 1982.

CHAPTER 13

Studying Adolescence: Research Methods and Issues

CHAPTER OUTLINE

Research Strategies

Number of Subjects
Degree of Control

Issues and Designs in Developmental Research

Cross-Sectional Designs
Longitudinal Designs
Sequential Designs
Path Analysis

Response Measures in Developmental Research

Dependent Variables
Types of Response Measures

Research Issues

Internal and External Validity
Theory-Guided Research
Operationalizing Concepts
Sampling
Bias and Blind Controls
Tests of Significance
Ethics

Research Designs

Between-Subjects Designs
Within-Subjects Designs
Matched-Subjects Designs
Factorial Designs

KEY TERMS

Case Study
Self-Report
Archival Research
Naturalistic Observation
Quasi-Experimental Designs
Confounding
Testing Effect
History Effect
Statistical Regression
Experiment
Random Assignment
Independent Variable
Reliability
Validity
Sensitivity

Direct Observation
Projective Measures
Internal Validity
External Validity
Operational Definition
Population
Sample
Bias
Double-Blind Controls
Dependent Variable
Correlational Research
Classification Variable
Age Changes
Cohort Differences
Time of Measurement Differences

Cross-Sectional Designs
Longitudinal Designs
Subject Mortality
Sequential Designs
Path Analysis
Test of Significance
Degrees of Freedom
Between-Subjects Designs
Within-Subjects Designs
Carryover Effects
Order Effects
Matched-Subjects Designs
Factorial Designs
Main Effect
Interaction

LEARNING OBJECTIVES

After reading the chapter, you should be able to:

1. Distinguish research strategies in terms of the number of subjects studied and the degree of control over conditions that could affect observations.

2. Discuss confounds common to **quasi-experimental designs.**

3. Discuss the importance of **random assignment** for causal inferences in experiments.

4. Distinguish **experiments** from **correlational research.**

5. Distinguish **age changes, cohort differences** and **time of measurement effects.**

6. Compare **cross-sectional, longitudinal,** and **sequential designs** in terms of their ability to distinguish age changes from potential confounds.

7. Summarize different types of response measures.

8. Distinguish **internal** and **external validity.**

9. Discuss **between-subjects, within-subjects,** and **matched-subjects designs.**

10. Define an **interaction.**

CLASS ACTIVITIES

Activity 13-1   Comparison of Popular and Scientific Approaches to Problems

Have students clip an article on an adolescent problem behavior (for example, teenage pregnancy, use of cigarettes/alcohol, delinquency) from the newspaper and compare this with the way the same topic is treated in a research article published in a scientific journal.

Activity 13-2   Role-Playing Informing Human Subjects of Their Rights

Have students break into small groups in which they role-play a researcher and participants in a project in which they will be asked to disclose intimate information in the presence of others (or some other scenario) and may be reluctant to participate.

SUGGESTED READINGS

Brannigan, G. G., & Merrens, M. R. (1993). *The undaunted psychologist.* San Francisco: McGraw-Hill.

Cozby, P. C. (1993). *Methods in behavioral research* (5th ed.). Mountain View, CA: Mayfield.

Ware, M. E., & Brewere, C. L. (1988). *Handbook for teaching statistics and research methods.* Lawrence Erlbaum.

AUDIOVISUALS

1. *Hypothesis Testing: Rats, Robots, and Roller Skates.* color / 27 min / film. Presents principles of hypothesis testing and use of experimental controls in conducting research; uses humor to illustrate basic principles. Kent State, 1975.

2. *Methodology: The Psychologist and the Experiment.* color / 30 min / film. Presents research methodology and illustrates the logic of conducting an experiment. Penn State, 1975.

1 Population Pyramids for the Years 1982, 2000, 2030, and 2080

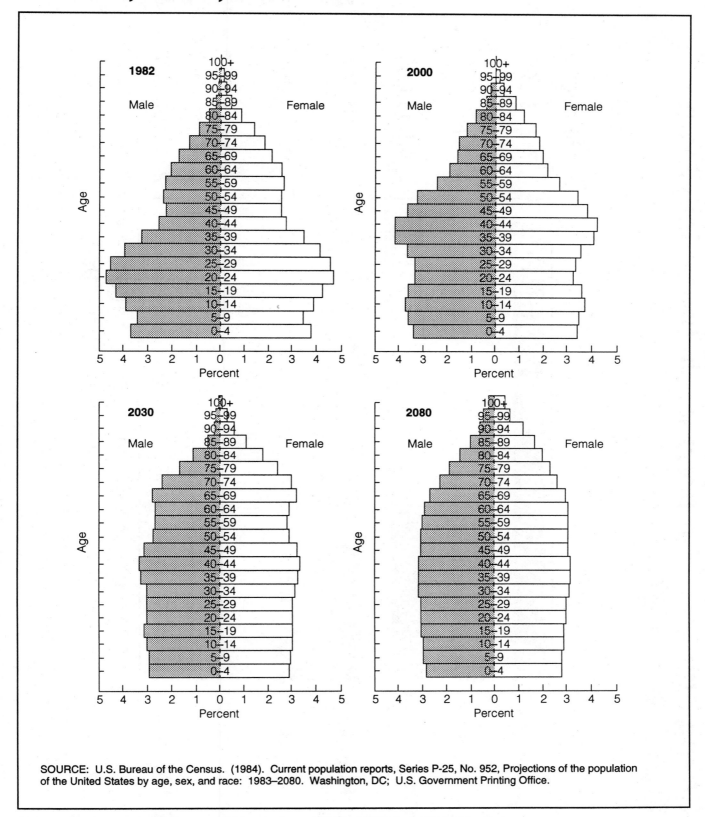

SOURCE: U.S. Bureau of the Census. (1984). Current population reports, Series P-25, No. 952, Projections of the population of the United States by age, sex, and race: 1983–2080. Washington, DC; U.S. Government Printing Office.

2 Changing Ethnic Compostion in the United States From 1980 to1990

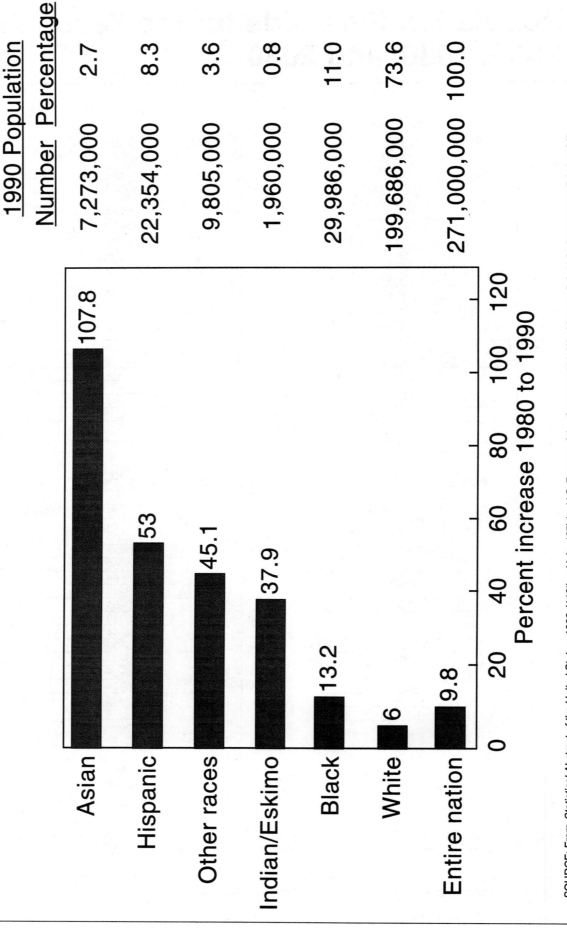

	1990 Population	
	Number	Percentage
Asian	7,273,000	2.7
Hispanic	22,354,000	8.3
Other races	9,805,000	3.6
Indian/Eskimo	1,960,000	0.8
Black	29,986,000	11.0
White	199,686,000	73.6
Entire nation	271,000,000	100.0

Percent increase 1980 to 1990

Asian 107.8
Hispanic 53
Other races 45.1
Indian/Eskimo 37.9
Black 13.2
White 6
Entire nation 9.8

SOURCE: From *Statistical Abstract of the United States: 1992* (112th ed.) (p. 187) by U.S. Bureau of the Census, 1992, Washington, DC: U.S. Government Printing Office.

Cobb, *Adolescence, Continuity, Change, and Diversity,* Second Edition, ©1995 Mayfield Publishing Company

3 Gender-Biased Language

HE	SHE
Discussed	Chattered
Reminded	Nagged
Networked	Gossiped
Complained	Bitched
Is forgetful	Is an airhead
Is confident	Is conceited
Is careful	Is picky
Is articulate	Is talkative
Has character lines	Has wrinkles
Is assertive	Is pushy
Was tired	Was depressed
Was upset	Was emotional
Dressed nicely	Dressed "to kill"
Was friendly	Was flirting
Was upset	Was moody

SOURCE: Based in part on *Sex Differences in Human Communication* (p. 131) by B. W. Eakins and R. G. Eakins, 1978, Boston: Houghton Mifflin, Copyright 1978 by B. W. Eakins and R. G. Eakins. Adapted by permission.

4 Developmental Tasks: Infancy and Early Childhood

- Learning to walk

- Learning to take solid foods

- Learning to talk

- Learning to control the elimination of body wastes

- Learning sex differences and sexual modesty

- Forming concepts and learning language to describe social and physical reality

- Getting ready to read

SOURCE: R. J. Havighurst. (1972). *Developmental tasks and education.* New York: David McKay.

5 Developmental Tasks: Middle Childhood

- Learning physical skills necessary for ordinary games

- Building wholesome attitudes toward oneself

- Learning to get along with age-mates

- Learning appropriate masculine or feminine social roles

- Learning fundamental skills in reading, writing, and calculating

- Developing concepts necessary for everyday living

- Developing conscience, morality, and a scale of values

- Achieving personal independence

- Developing attitudes toward social groups and institutions

SOURCE: R. J. Havighurst. (1972). *Developmental tasks and education.* New York: David McKay.

6 Developmental Tasks: Adolescence

- Achieving new and more mature relations with age-mates of both sexes

- Achieving a masculine or feminine social role

- Accepting one's physique and using the body effectively

- Achieving emotional independence from parents and other adults

- Preparing for marriage and family life

- Preparing for an economic career

- Acquiring a set of values and an ethical system as a guide to behavior—developing an ideology

- Desiring and achieving socially responsible behavior

SOURCE: R. J. Havighurst. (1972). *Developmental tasks and education.* New York: David McKay.

7 Developmental Tasks: Early Adulthood

- Selecting a mate

- Learning to live with a marriage partner

- Starting a family

- Rearing children

- Managing a home

- Getting started in an occupation

- Taking on civic responsibility

- Finding a congenial social group

SOURCE: R. J. Havighurst. (1972). *Developmental tasks and education.* New York: David McKay.

8 Developmental Tasks: Middle Age

- Assisting teenaged children to become responsible and happy adults

- Achieving adult social and civic responsibility

- Reaching and maintaining satisfactory performance in one's occupational career

- Developing adult leisure-time activities

- Relating oneself to one's spouse as a person

- Accepting and adjusting to the physiological changes of middle age

- Adjusting to aging parents

SOURCE: R. J. Havighurst. (1972). *Developmental tasks and education.* New York: David McKay.

9 Developmental Tasks: Later Maturity

- Adjusting to decreasing physical strength and health

- Adjusting to retirement and reduced income

- Adjusting to the death of a spouse

- Establishing an explicit affiliation with one's age group

- Adopting and adapting social roles in a flexible way

- Establishing satisfactory physical living arrangements

SOURCE: R. J. Havighurst. (1972). *Developmental tasks and education*. New York: David McKay.

10 Characteristics of a Good Theory

- **Ability to Account for Data**
  Theory must account for existing data and well-established facts within its domain.

- **Explanatory Relevance**
  Theoretical explanation must offer good grounds for believing that the phenomenon would occur under specified conditions.

- **Testability**
  A theory must be testable. That is, it must be capable of failing some empirical test.

- **Prediction of Novel Events**
  A theory should predict phenomena the theory was not specifically designed to account for, but which are within its domain.

- **Parsimony**
  A theory should explain phenomena within its domain with the fewest possible assumptions.

11 Comparison of Developmental Models

	Environmental	Organismic	Psychodynamic
Organism is	Passive	Active	Active
Behavior is	Reactive, involuntary	Organized, voluntary	Organized, determined
Process of	Behavioral conditioning	Environmental-genetic interactions	Environmental-genetic interactions
Focus on	Behavior	Cognition, perception	Intrapsychic dynamics
Stages	No	Yes	Yes

Cobb, *Adolescence, Continuity, Change, and Diversity*, Second Edition, ©1995 Mayfield Publishing Company

12 Erikson's Developmental Stages

Stage	Psychosocial Crisis
Birth to Adolescence	
Infancy	Trust vs. mistrust Realization that needs will be met leads to trust in others and self
Toddlerhood	Autonomy vs. shame and doubt Physical maturation gives sense of being able to do things for self
Early childhood	Initiative vs. guilt Increasing abilities promote exploration and expand experience
Middle Childhood	Industry vs. inferiority Accomplishments and skills provide basis for self-esteem
Adolescence to Old Age	
Adolescence	Identity vs. identity diffusion Biological and social changes of adolescence occasion a search for continuity of self
Early adulthood	Intimacy vs. isolation Sense of self provides the basis for sexual and emotional intimacy with another adult
Middle adulthood	Generativity vs. stagnation Concern for children and future generations reflects need to leave something of oneself
Late adulthood	Integrity vs. despair Acceptance of one's life as having meaning gives one a sense of dignity

SOURCE: E. Erikson. (1963). *Childhood and society.* New York: Norton

Cobb, *Adolescence, Continuity, Change, and Diversity,* Second Edition, ©1995 Mayfield Publishing Company

13 Gilligan's Analysis of Gender Differences

Females	Males
Developmental theme: Connectedness	Developomental theme: Separateness
Experiences self in relation to others	Experiences self as separate from others
Perspective regarding others: personal, as individuals with whom relationships reflect extensions of care	Perspective regarding others: formal, as members of a community in which interactions are regulated by rules
Views responsibility as doing something for others	Views responsibility as doing nothing to hurt others
Major strength: forming intimate relations with others	Major strength: functioning autonomously
Major weakness: functioning auto-nomously	Major weakness: forming intimate relations with others

SOURCE: Carol Gilligan. (1982). *In a Different Voice.* Cambridge, Mass.: Harvard University Press.

14 Effects of Hormones on Physical Development and Sexual Maturation at Puberty

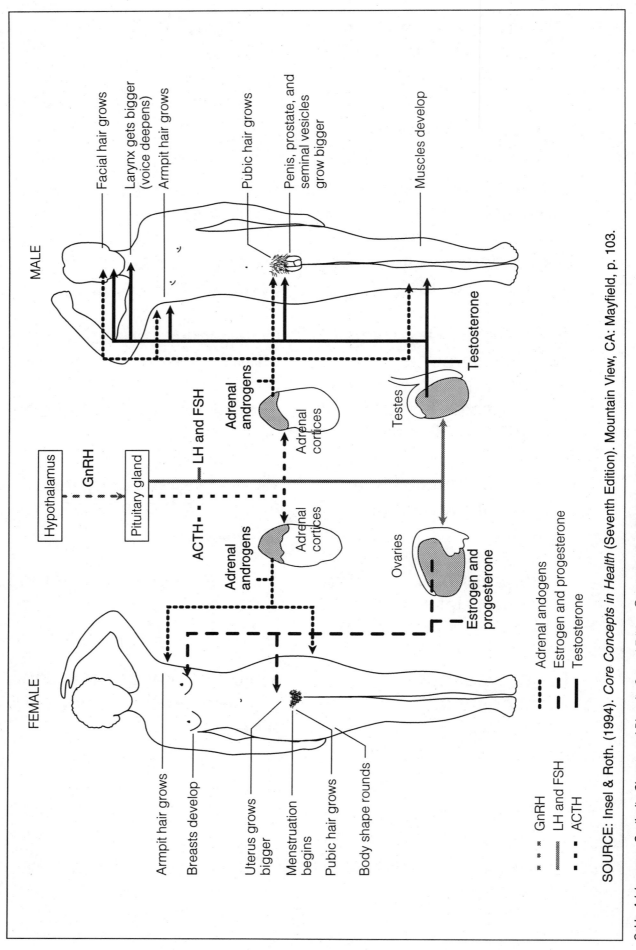

SOURCE: Insel & Roth. (1994). *Core Concepts in Health* (Seventh Edition). Mountain View, CA: Mayfield, p. 103.

Cobb, *Adolescence, Continuity, Change, and Diversity*, Second Edition, © 1995 Mayfield Publishing Company

15 Sequence of Changes at Puberty

Girls			Boys		
Characteristic	**Age of first appearance (Years)**	**Major hormonal influence**	**Characteristic**	**Age of first appearance (years)**	**Major hormonal influence**
1. Growth of breasts	8–13	Pituitary growth hormone, estrogen, progesterone, thyroxine	1. Growth of testes, scrotal sac	10–13.5	Pituitary growth hormone, testosterone
2. Growth of pubic hair	8–14	Adrenal androgen	2. Growth of pubic hair	10–15	Testosterone
3. Body growth	9.5–14.5	Pituitary growth hormone, adrenal androgen, estrogen	3. Body growth	10.5–16	Pituitary growth hormone, testosterone
4. Menarche	10–16.5	Hypothalamic releasing factors, FSH, LH, estrogen, progesterone	4. Growth of penis	11–14.5	Testosterone
5. Underarm hair	About two years after pubic hair	Adrenal androgens	5. Change in voice (growth of larynx)	About the same time as penis growth	Testosterone
6. Oil- and sweat-producing glands (acne occurs when glands are clogged)	About the same time as underarm hair	Adrenal androgens	6. Facial and underarm hair	About two years after pubic hair appears	Testosterone
			7. Oil- and sweat-producing glands, acne	About the same time as underarm hair	Testosterone

SOURCE: B. Goldstein. (1976). *Introduction to human sexuality.* Belmont, CA: Star.

Cobb, *Adolescence, Continuity, Change, and Diversity,* Second Edition, ©1995 Mayfield Publishing Company

16 Percentage of High School Students Who Have Had Sexual Intercourse: Gender

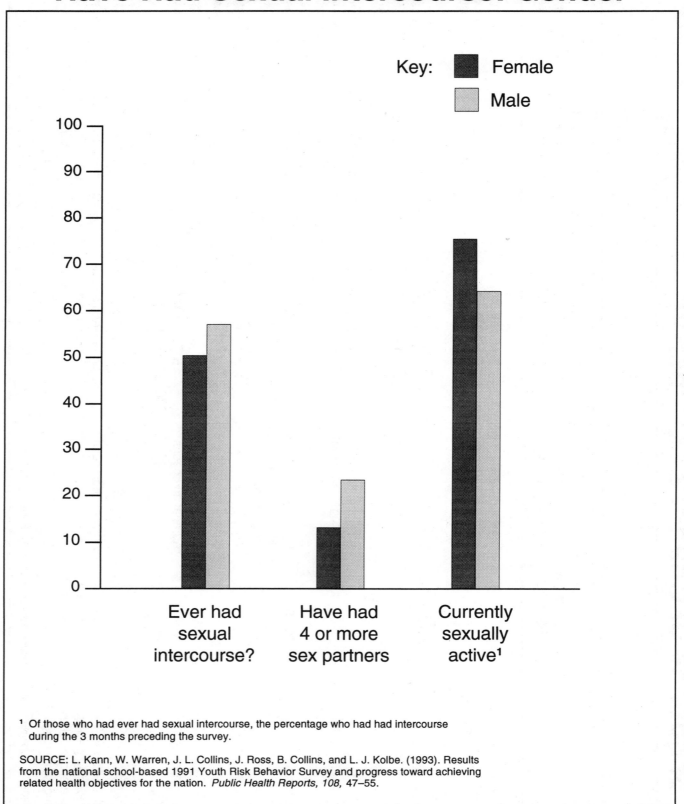

Key:
- Female
- Male

Categories (x-axis):
- Ever had sexual intercourse?
- Have had 4 or more sex partners
- Currently sexually active[1]

[1] Of those who had ever had sexual intercourse, the percentage who had had intercourse during the 3 months preceding the survey.

SOURCE: L. Kann, W. Warren, J. L. Collins, J. Ross, B. Collins, and L. J. Kolbe. (1993). Results from the national school-based 1991 Youth Risk Behavior Survey and progress toward achieving related health objectives for the nation. *Public Health Reports, 108,* 47–55.

17 Percentage of High School Students Who Have Had Sexual Intercourse: Grade

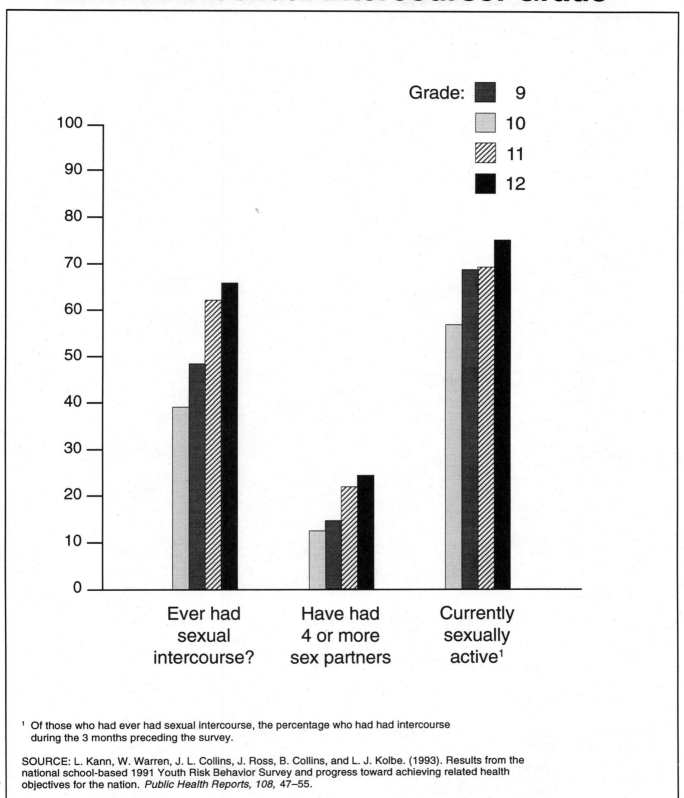

Grade:
■ 9
□ 10
▨ 11
■ 12

¹ Of those who had ever had sexual intercourse, the percentage who had had intercourse during the 3 months preceding the survey.

SOURCE: L. Kann, W. Warren, J. L. Collins, J. Ross, B. Collins, and L. J. Kolbe. (1993). Results from the national school-based 1991 Youth Risk Behavior Survey and progress toward achieving related health objectives for the nation. *Public Health Reports, 108,* 47–55.

18 Percentage of High School Students Who Have Had Sexual Intercourse: Ethnicity

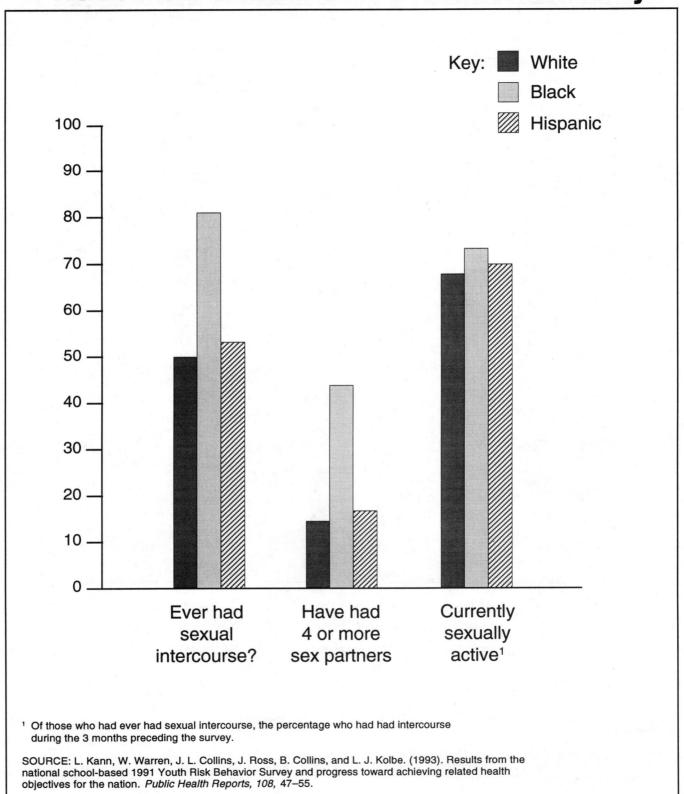

¹ Of those who had ever had sexual intercourse, the percentage who had had intercourse during the 3 months preceding the survey.

SOURCE: L. Kann, W. Warren, J. L. Collins, J. Ross, B. Collins, and L. J. Kolbe. (1993). Results from the national school-based 1991 Youth Risk Behavior Survey and progress toward achieving related health objectives for the nation. *Public Health Reports, 108,* 47–55.

19 Percentage of Others Believed to Be Sexually Active as a Function of Personal Sexual Activity

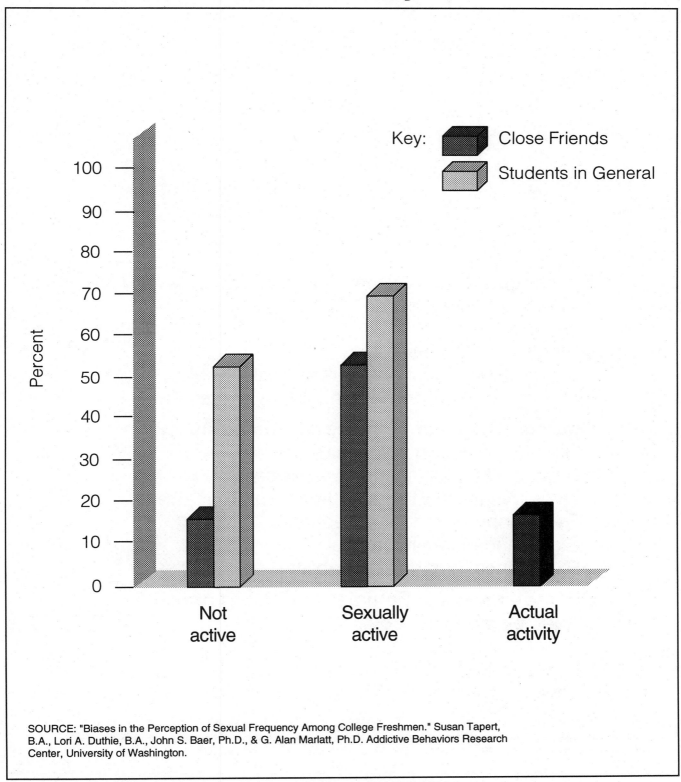

SOURCE: "Biases in the Perception of Sexual Frequency Among College Freshmen." Susan Tapert, B.A., Lori A. Duthie, B.A., John S. Baer, Ph.D., & G. Alan Marlatt, Ph.D. Addictive Behaviors Research Center, University of Washington.

20 Decision Making about Pregnancy Resolution

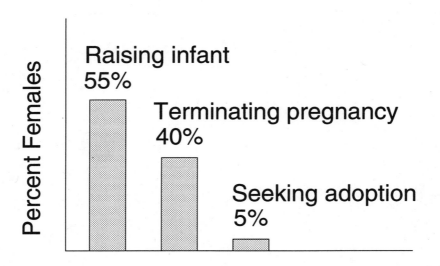

Characteristics of Females Choosing to Give Birth:
Age: mid-adolescence (15-18)
Non-white
Single parent families
Lower educational and career goals
Higher involvement with the father of the infant

Characteristics of Females Choosing Adoption:
Higher socioeconomic status
Higher educational and career goals
Lives in suburban-rural rather than urban areas
Feels unprepared for parenthood
Experiences family pressure
Experiences financial instability

Characteristics of Females Choosing Abortion:
Age: below 15 and over 18
Intact families
Higher educational and career goals
Lower involvement with the father of the infant

SOURCE: K. McCluskey-Fawcett. (1991). Briefing: Adolescent pregnancy and parenting. The Psychology Teacher Network, 1, 2–4. © 1991 by the American Psychological Association. Adapted by permission.

21 Eating Disorders

Anorexia nervosa is characterized by:

- Refusal to reach and maintain body weight over a minimal normal weight for age and height
- Intense fear of gaining weight or becoming fat, even though underweight
- Disturbance in the way in which body weight, size, or shape is experienced or perceived
- In females, absence of at least three consecutive menstrual cycles when otherwise expected to occur

Anorexia is most prevalent among females, particularly in the middle and upper social classes. It affects between 1 and 3 million Americans, ending in death between 15 and 20 percent of the time.

Bulimia is characterized by

- Recurrent episodes of binge eating
- A feeling of lack of control over eating behavior during the eating binges
- Regularly engaging in either self-induced vomiting, use of laxatives or diuretics, strict dieting or fasting, or vigorous exercise in order to prevent weight gain
- A minimum average of two binge eating episodes a week for at least three months
- Persistent overconcern with body shape and weight

Like anorexia, bulimia affects women from upper socioeconomic classes the most.

Cobb, *Adolescence, Continuity, Change, and Diversity,* Second Edition, ©1995 Mayfield Publishing Company

22 Piaget's Four Stages of Cognitive Development

Stage	Qualities of Thought
Sensorimotor (birth to 2 yrs)	Repetition of innate reflexes forms basis for coordinated, intentional actions. Infant awareness limited to its senses and actions; symbolic representation develops late in infancy.
Preoperational (2 to 6–7 yrs)	Representational skills develop. Child masters language, imagery, drawing but can use these only to reflect the world from its own perspective. Attention is narrowly focused, and child may miss important information. Can represent static situations, not changes in these.
Concrete Operational (6–7 to 11 yrs)	Can represent tranformations as well as static properties of objects. Can adopt another's perspective. Problem solving limited to consideration of actual properties of objects.
Formal Operational (11 yrs and on)	Can solve problems by considering all possible outcomes, even those not physically possible. Thought characterized by abstract reasoning.

SOURCE: R. S. Siegler. (1986). *Children's thinking.* Englewood Cliffs, NJ: Prentice-Hall, pp. 24–25.

23 Percentage of Individuals at Different Points from the Mean IQ of 100

IQ	Classification	Percent Included*
130 and above	Very superior	2.6%
120-129	Superior	6.9
110-119	High average	16.6
90-109	Average	49.1
80-89	Low average	16.1
70-79	Borderline	6.4
69 and below	Mentally retarded	2.3

Cobb, *Adolescence, Continuity, Change, and Diversity*, Second Edition, ©1995 Mayfield Publishing Company

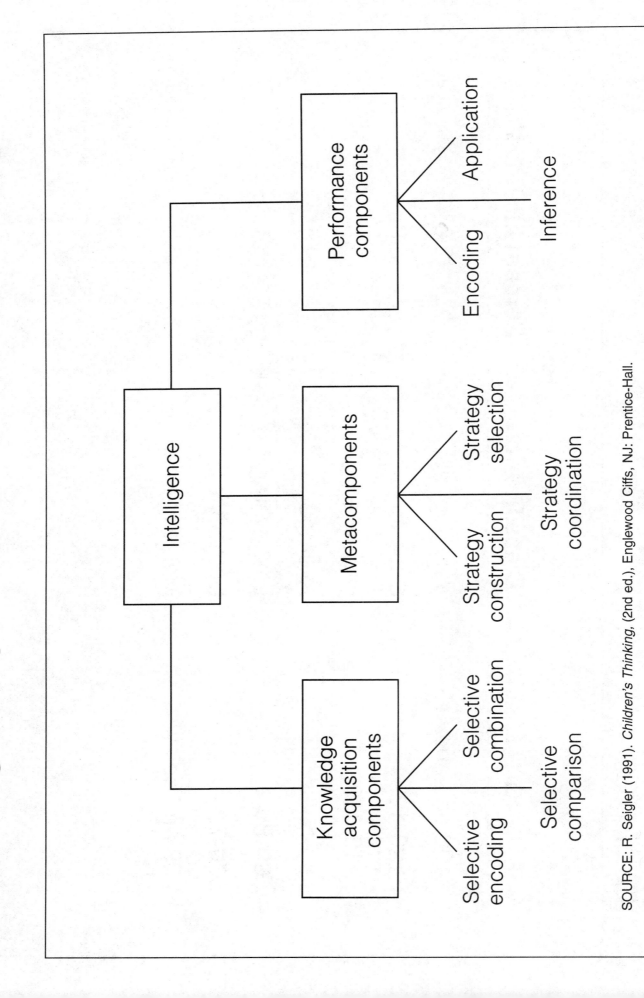

SOURCE: R. Seigler (1991). *Children's Thinking*, (2nd ed.), Englewood Cliffs, NJ: Prentice-Hall.

25 Gardner's Seven Forms of Intelligence

Form of Intelligence	Potential Professions
Musical	Musician Music teacher
Body-kinesthetic	Dancer Athlete
Logical-mathematical	Scientist Mathematician Teacher
Linguistic	Interpreter
Spatial	Artist Architect Landscape designer
Interpersonal (understanding others)	Psychologist Counselor
Intrapersonal (understanding the self)	Poet Writer

SOURCE: H. Gardner. (1983). *Frames of mind.* New York: Basic Books

26 Family Stress and Family Satisfaction

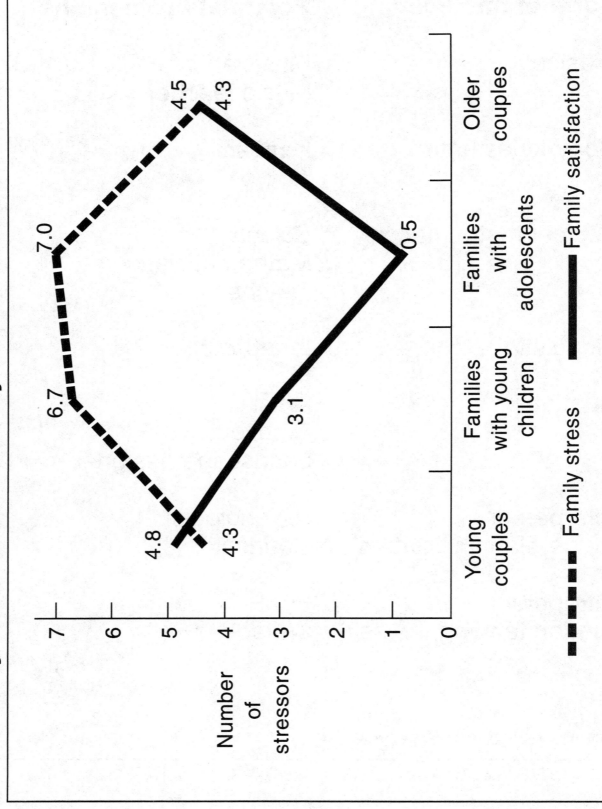

Source: From *Families: What Makes Them Work* (2nd ed.) (pp. 122, 181) by D. H. Olson, H. I. McCubbin, H. Barnes, A. Larsen, M. Muxen, and M. Wilson, 1989, Los Angeles: Sage. Copyright 1989 by Sage Publications. Reprinted by permission.

Cobb, Adolescence, Continuity, Change, and Diversity, Second Edition, ©1995 Mayfield Publishing Company

- About 90 percent of all Americans marry at some time in their lives (U.S. Bureau of the Census, 1992).

- In 1991, there were 2,371,000 marriages and 1,187,000 divorces (U.S. Bureau of the Census, 1991).

- People marrying today have a 50 to 55 percent chance of divorcing (Glick, 1989).

- The median age for first marriage is 25.5 for men and 23.7 for women (U.S. Bureau of the Census, 1991).

- The average age of remarriage for men is 37 years and for women,

- 33.6 (U.S. Bureau of the Census, 1992).

- First marriages for both the bride and groom account for only 54 percent of the marriages each year (U.S. Bureau of the Census, 1991).

- Most divorces involve children, and more than 1 million children are affected by divorce each year in the United States (Glick, 1989).

- Most divorced individuals eventually remarry. For younger divorced individuals, this remarriage occurs within five years of the divorce (U.S. Bureau of the Census, 1992).

28 Communication Patterns That Foster Individuation: Individuality

INDIVIDUALITY

Self-Assertion: The ability to have one's own ideas and express them.

"I'd like to see the pyramids in Mexico."

Separateness: The ability to say how one differs from others.

1. Requests action: "All right, let's vote on this."
2. Directly disagrees: "Get real, Mom. Do you think you can get us to sweat a path through the jungle once we've seen the sand of Acapulco?
3. Indirectly disagrees: "Do you know how hot it is in Florida in August?"
4. Irrelevant comment: "They're alligators, not crocodiles, Surfer Joe."

SOURCE: C. Cooper, H. Grotevant, and S. Condon. (1983). Individuality and connectedness in the family as a context for adolescent identity formation and role-taking skill. In H. D. Grotevant and C. R. Cooper (Eds.), *Adolescent development in the family.* San Francisco: Jossey-Bass.

CONNECTEDNESS

Permeability: Openness and responsiveness to the opinions of others.

1. Acknowledges: "Hmm."
2. Requests information or validation: "How far inland are they?"
3. Agrees with another's ideas: "I could sure use some time on a beach."
4. Relevant comment: "Maybe we should think of a winter vacation."
5. Complies with a request: "Okay, let's vote."

Mutuality: Sensitivity and respect for others' ideas.

1. Indirect suggestion of action: "Why don't we visit Grandma and then go someplace exotic like the Everglades?"
2. Compromise: "I'd like to see the pyramids in Mexico. We could stop off at Acapulco on the way."
3. States other's feelings: "Willie'd die in the heat there, too."
4. Answers request for information/validation: "I don't know, but I could call a travel agent."

SOURCE: C. Cooper, H. Grotevant, and S. Condon. (1983). Individuality and connectedness in the family as a context for adolescent identity formation and role-taking skill. In H. D. Grotevant and C. R. Cooper (Eds.), *Adolescent development in the family.* San Francisco: Jossey-Bass.

30 Frequencies of Conflicts Between Adolescents and Parents

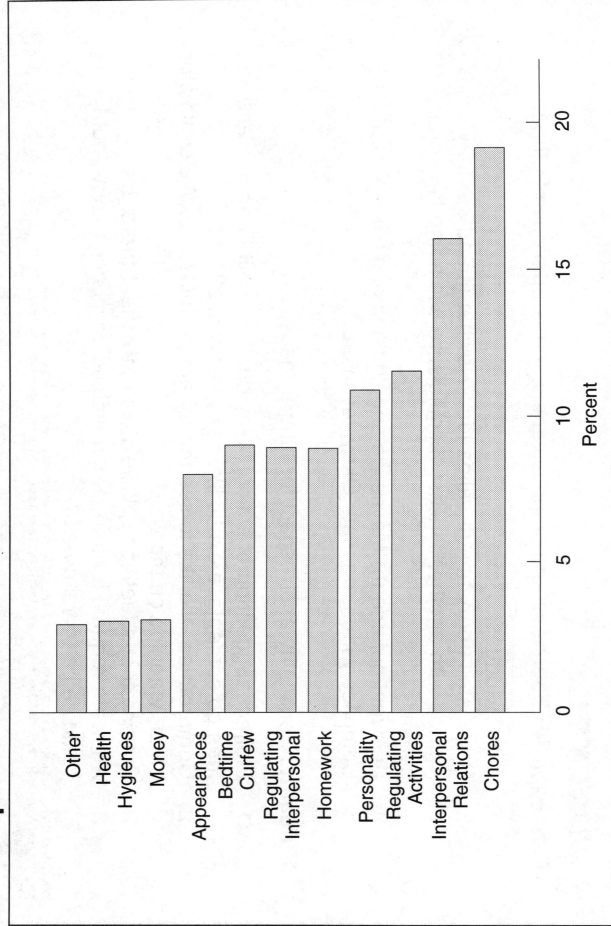

SOURCE: J. G. Smetana, J. L. Braeges, and J. Yau. (1991). Doing what you say and saying what you do: Reasoning about adolescent-parent conflict in interviews and interactions. Journal of Adolescent Research, 6, 276–295. ©1991 by Sage Publications. Reprinted by permission of Sage Publications, Inc.

Parenting Styles and Social Competence

Parenting Style	Characteristics	Adolescent Social Behavior
Authoritarian	Punitive, restrictive, controlling	Ineffective social interaction; inactive
Authoritative	Encourages independence; warm and nurturing; control with explanation; adolescent expresses views	Social competence and responsibility
Permissive	Lack of involvement; nonpunitive; few demands; adolescent has a lot of freedom	Immature; poor self-restraint; poor leader-ship

SOURCE: Adapted from D. Baumrind. (1971). *Current patterns of parental authority.* Developmental Psychology Monographs, 4, 1.

Cobb, *Adolescence, Continuity, Change, and Diversity,* Second Edition, ©1995 Mayfield Publishing Company

32 Percentage of Time Spent with Friends, Family, Classmates, or Alone

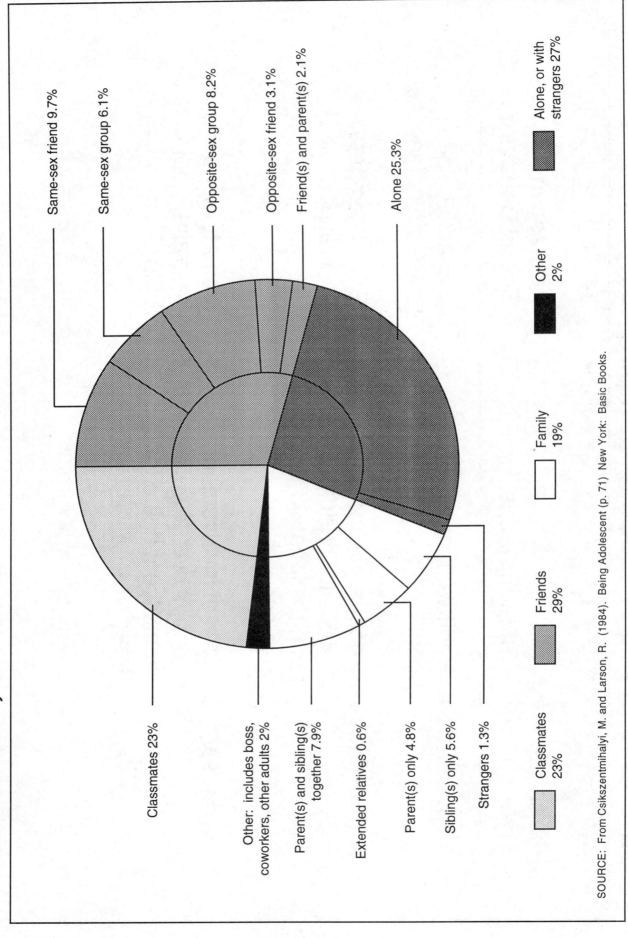

Same-sex friend 9.7%

Same-sex group 6.1%

Opposite-sex group 8.2%

Opposite-sex friend 3.1%

Friend(s) and parent(s) 2.1%

Alone 25.3%

Classmates 23%

Other: includes boss, coworkers, other adults 2%

Parent(s) and sibling(s) together 7.9%

Extended relatives 0.6%

Parent(s) only 4.8%

Sibling(s) only 5.6%

Strangers 1.3%

Alone, or with strangers 27%

Other 2%

Family 19%

Friends 29%

Classmates 23%

SOURCE: From Csikszentmihalyi, M. and Larson, R. (1984). *Being Adolescent* (p. 71) New York: Basic Books.

Cobb, *Adolescence, Continuity, Change, and Diversity,* Second Edition, ©1995 Mayfield Publishing Company

33 How Adolescents Spend Their Time

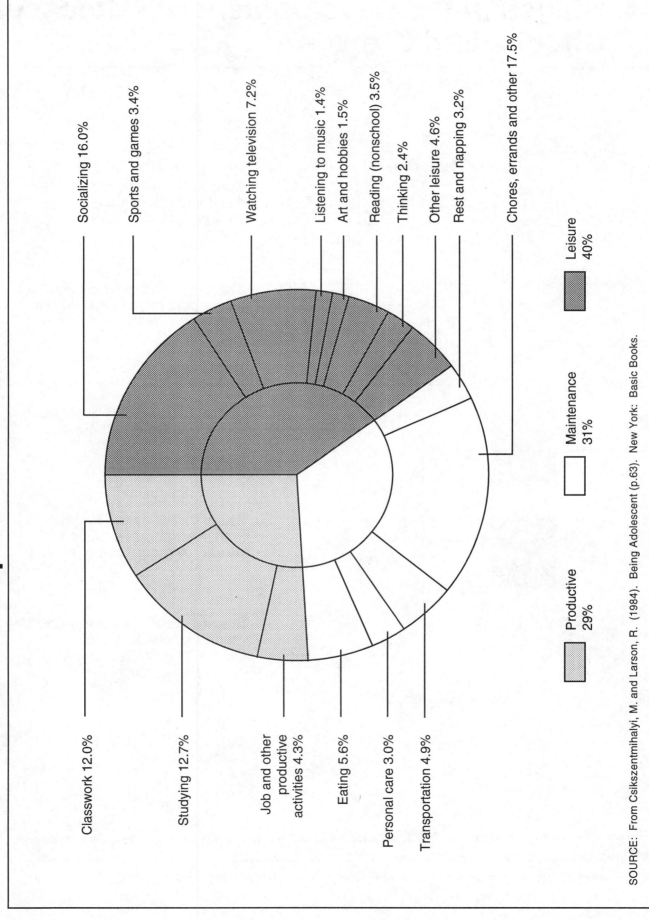

Socializing 16.0%

Sports and games 3.4%

Watching television 7.2%

Listening to music 1.4%

Art and hobbies 1.5%

Reading (nonschool) 3.5%

Thinking 2.4%

Other leisure 4.6%

Rest and napping 3.2%

Chores, errands and other 17.5%

Classwork 12.0%

Studying 12.7%

Job and other productive activities 4.3%

Eating 5.6%

Personal care 3.0%

Transportation 4.9%

Productive 29%

Maintenance 31%

Leisure 40%

SOURCE: From Csikszentmihalyi, M. and Larson, R. (1984). Being Adolescent (p.63). New York: Basic Books.

Cobb, *Adolescence, Continuity, Change, and Diversity*, Second Edition, ©1995 Mayfield Publishing Company

34 Stages in the Development of Adolescent Cliques and Crowds

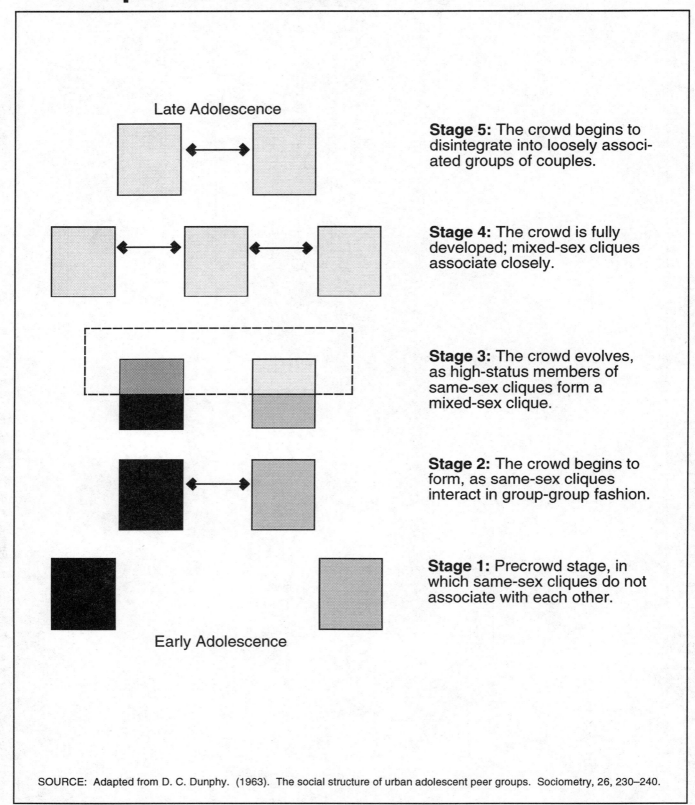

Late Adolescence

Stage 5: The crowd begins to disintegrate into loosely associated groups of couples.

Stage 4: The crowd is fully developed; mixed-sex cliques associate closely.

Stage 3: The crowd evolves, as high-status members of same-sex cliques form a mixed-sex clique.

Stage 2: The crowd begins to form, as same-sex cliques interact in group-group fashion.

Stage 1: Precrowd stage, in which same-sex cliques do not associate with each other.

Early Adolescence

SOURCE: Adapted from D. C. Dunphy. (1963). The social structure of urban adolescent peer groups. Sociometry, 26, 230–240.

35 Physical Features Noticed When Meeting a Person of the Other Sex

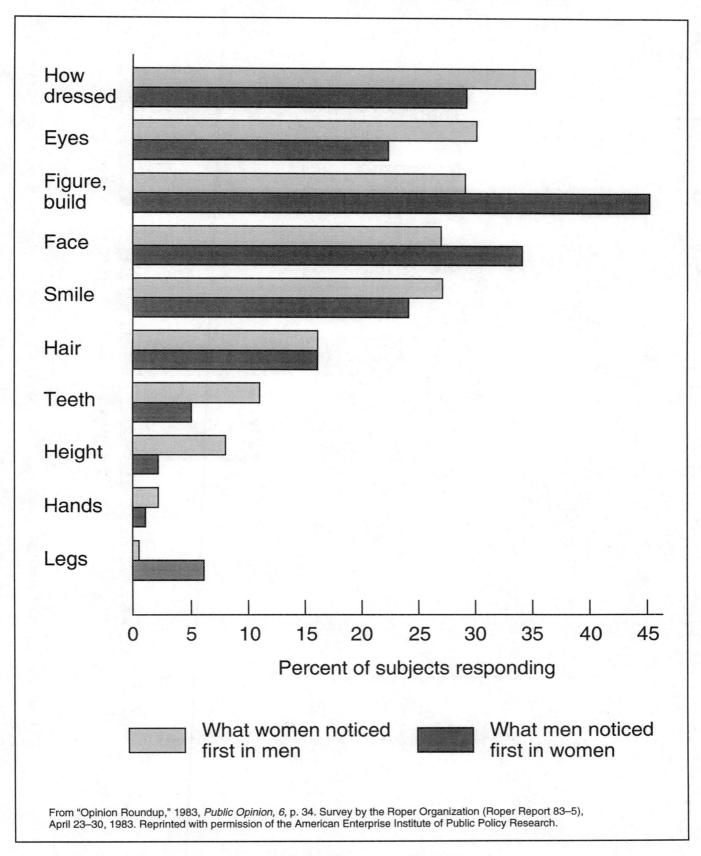

Percent of subjects responding

What women noticed first in men   What men noticed first in women

From "Opinion Roundup," 1983, *Public Opinion, 6,* p. 34. Survey by the Roper Organization (Roper Report 83–5), April 23–30, 1983. Reprinted with permission of the American Enterprise Institute of Public Policy Research.

36 Increase in High School Graduation Over the Past 100 Years

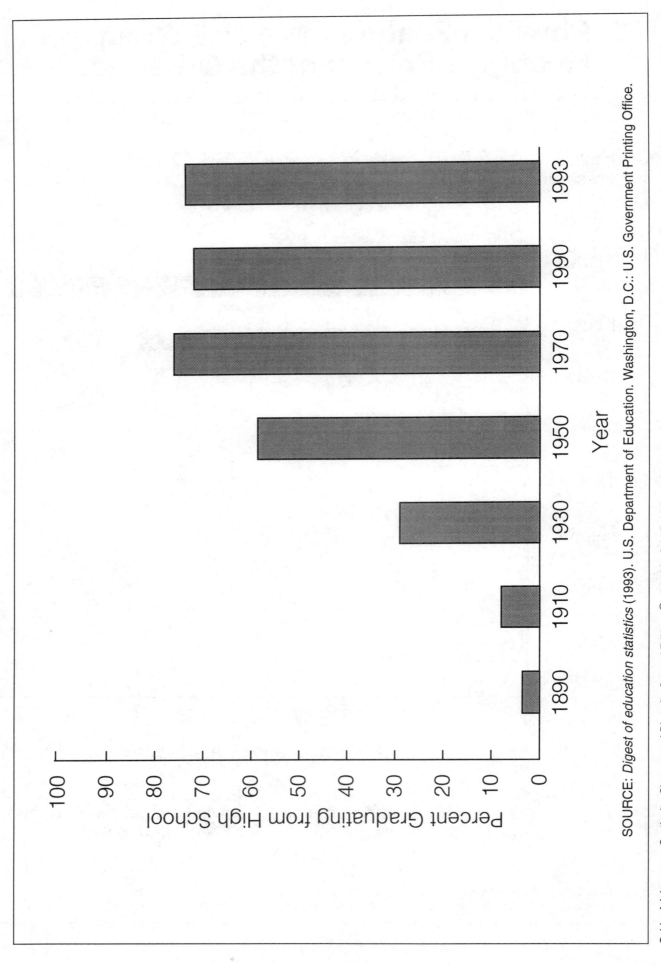

SOURCE: *Digest of education statistics* (1993). U.S. Department of Education. Washington, D.C.: U.S. Government Printing Office.

Cobb, *Adolescence, Continuity, Change, and Diversity*, Second Edition, © 1995 Mayfield Publishing Company

Teachers' Ratings of Top Disciplinary Problems— Then and Now

1940

Talking out of turn
Chewing gum
Making noise
Running in the halls
Cutting in line
Dress-code violations
Littering

1990

Drug Abuse
Alcohol abuse
Pregnancy
Suicide
Rape
Robbery
Assault

SOURCE: Toch, T. (1993). Violence in schools. *U.S. News & World Report, 115*, 31-37.

Cobb, *Adolescence, Continuity, Change, and Diversity,* Second Edition, ©1995 Mayfield Publishing Company

38 Percentage of Adolescents Experiencing Violence at School: 8th Grade

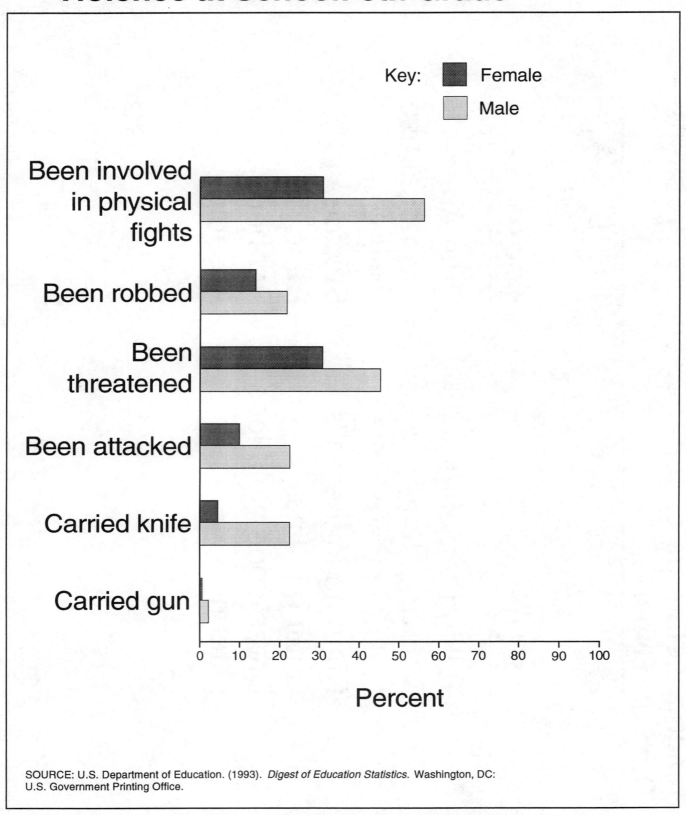

Key: Female Male

Been involved in physical fights

Been robbed

Been threatened

Been attacked

Carried knife

Carried gun

Percent

0 10 20 30 40 50 60 70 80 90 100

SOURCE: U.S. Department of Education. (1993). *Digest of Education Statistics.* Washington, DC: U.S. Government Printing Office.

39 Percentage of Adolescents Experiencing Violence at School: 10th Grade

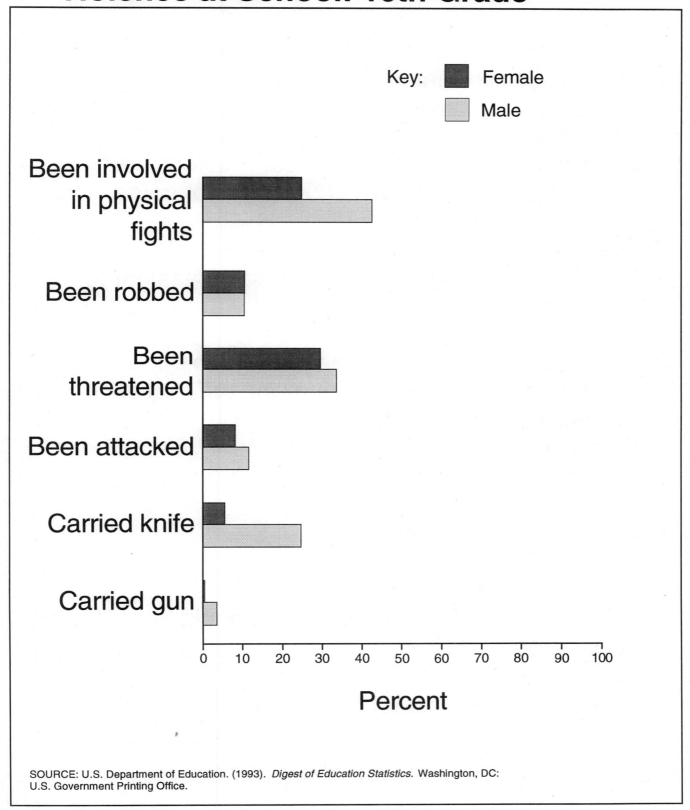

SOURCE: U.S. Department of Education. (1993). *Digest of Education Statistics*. Washington, DC: U.S. Government Printing Office.

Cobb, *Adolescence, Continuity, Change, and Diversity,* Second Edition, ©1995 Mayfield Publishing Company

40 Characteristics of Gifted Students

Asks many questions.
Has much information on many topics.
Adopts a questioning attitude.
Becomes unusually upset at injustices.
Is interested in social or political problems.
Has better reasons than you do for not doing what
  you want done.
Refuses to drill on repetitive tasks.
Becomes impatient when can't do an assignment
  perfectly.
Is a loner.
Is bored and frequently has nothing to do.
Completes part of an assignment and leaves it
  unfinished for something else.
Continues to work on an assignment when the rest
  of the class moves on to something else.
Is restless.
Daydreams.
Understands easily.
Likes to solve problems.
Has own ideas as to how things should be done.
Talks a lot.
Enjoys debate.
Enjoys abstract ideas.

SOURCE: B. Clark. (1988). Growing up gifted (3rd ed.). New York: Macmillan.

41 Marcia's Four Identity Statuses

EXPLORATION

	Present	Absent
Present	Identity Achieved	Identity Foreclosed
Absent	Moratorium	Identity Diffused

Commitment

42 Ego Identity and Adjustment Measures for Stages of Ethnic Identity

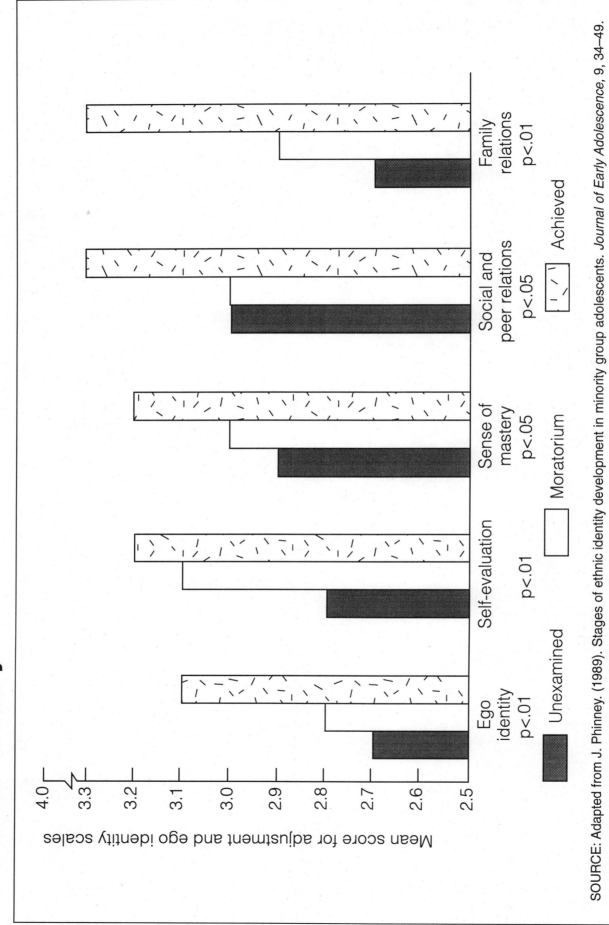

SOURCE: Adapted from J. Phinney. (1989). Stages of ethnic identity development in minority group adolescents. *Journal of Early Adolescence, 9,* 34–49.

43 Josselson's Dimensions of Relatedness and Their Pathological Poles

Absence	Dimension	Excess
Falling	Holding	Suffocation
Aloneness, loss	Attachment	Fearful clinging
Inhibition, emotional deadening	Passions	Obsessive love
Annihilation, rejection	Eye-to-eye validation	Transparency
Disillusionment, purposelessness	Idealization and identification	Slavish devotion
Loneliness	Mutuality and resonance	Merging
Alienation	Embeddedness	Over-conformity
Indifference	Tending (care)	Compulsive care giving

SOURCE: R. Josselson. (1992). *The space between us*. San Francisco: Jossey-Bass.

Cobb, *Adolescence, Continuity, Change, and Diversity*, Second Edition, ©1995 Mayfield Publishing Company

44 Intimacy Statuses in Adolescence

Isolated   Relationships consist only of casual acquaintances.

Stereotyped   Relationships are shallow and conventional.

Pseudointimate   Relationships are similar to those of Stereotyped, but have commitment to long-term sexual relationship; these defined through conventional roles rather than self disclosure.

Preintimate   Close, open relationships characterized by mutuality; ambivalence regarding commitment to long-term sexual relationship.

Intimate   Relationships are similar to those of Preintimate, but also have commitment to long-term sexual relationship.

SOURCE: D. C. Schiedel and J. E. Marcia. 1985. Ego identity, intimacy, sex role orientation, and gender. *Developmental Psychology, 21,* 149–160.

45 Relationship Between Dating Stage and Sexual Behaviors

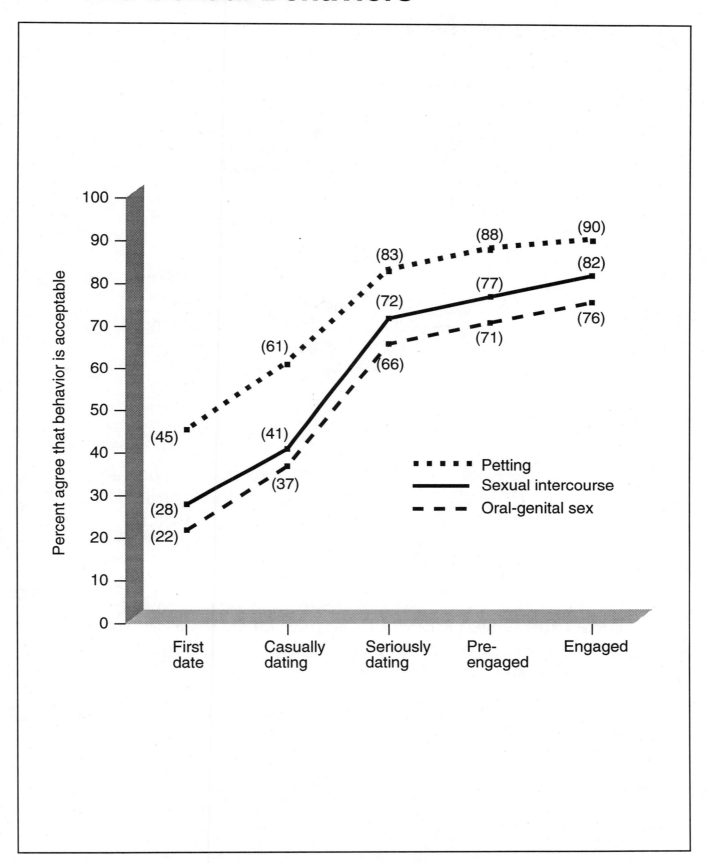

46 Date Rape

Recent Surveys Show:

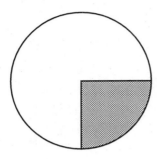 20-27% of U.S. female undergraduates have experienced rape

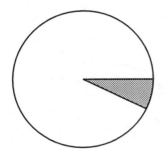 1 in 12 male students admitted to having fulfilled the prevailing definition of rape or attempted rape

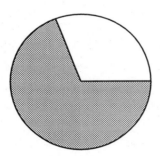 70% of all rapes reported are committed by men who know their victims

Date rape is also known as "acquaintance rape" because the rape may involve people who know each other or who may even be dating at the time.

(This information comes from surveys carried out at Kent State University, Cornell University, University of South Dakota, and North Carolina State University).

SOURCE: Insel/Roth, *Core Concepts in Health,* Fifth Edition, ©1988 Mayfield Publishing Company

47 Kensey's Continium of Sexual Orientation

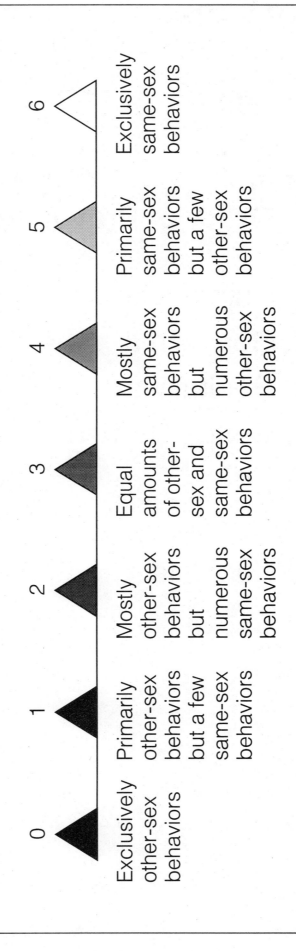

0	1	2	3	4	5	6
Exclusively other-sex behaviors	Primarily other-sex behaviors but a few same-sex behaviors	Mostly other-sex behaviors but numerous same-sex behaviors	Equal amounts of other-sex and same-sex behaviors	Mostly same-sex behaviors but numerous other-sex behaviors	Primarily same-sex behaviors but a few other-sex behaviors	Exclusively same-sex behaviors

SOURCE: B. Strong and C. DeVault (1994). *Human Sexuality.* Mountain View, CA: Mayfield.

Cobb, *Adolescence, Continuity, Change, and Diversity,* Second Edition, © 1995 Mayfield Publishing Company

Major Types of STDs in Order of Prevalence

1. Chlamydia
2. Gonorrhea
3. Genital warts
4. Genital herpes
5. HIV
6. Syphilis
7. Hepatitis

49 Rates of Infection for Men and Women after a Single Act of Intercourse with an Infected Partner

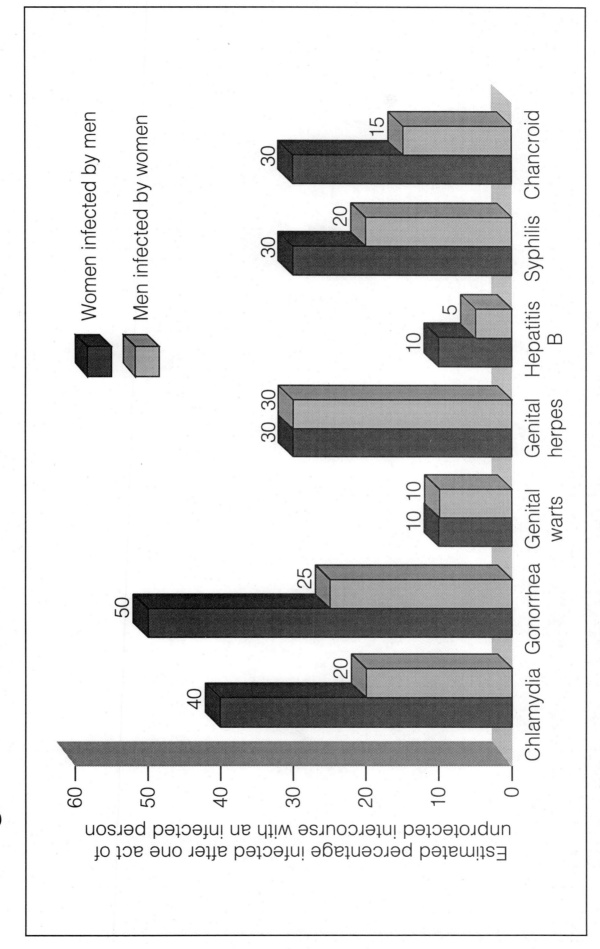

Cobb, *Adolescence, Continuity, Change, and Diversity*, Second Edition, ©1995 Mayfield Publishing Company

50 Distribution of AIDS Among Adolescents and Young Adults Ages 13–24 (Through June 1993)

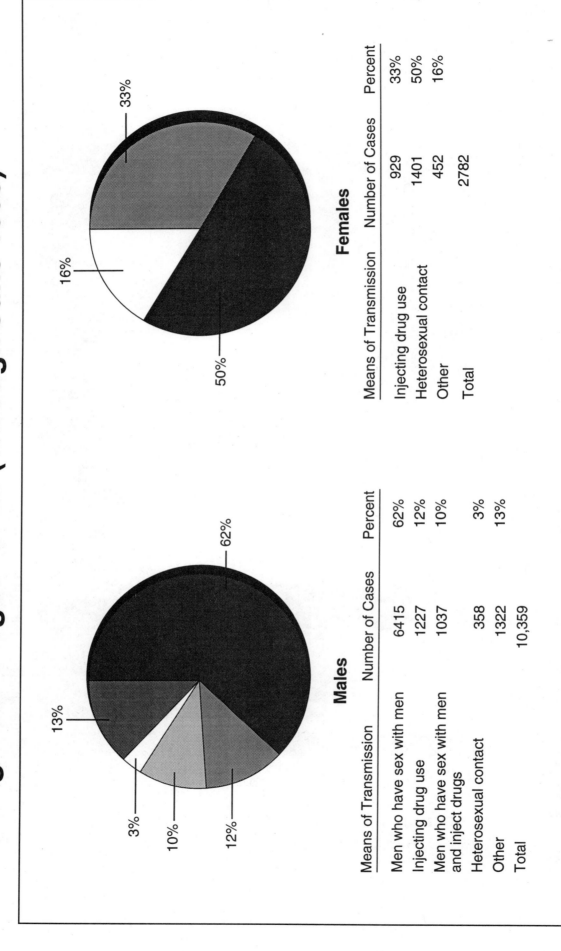

Males

Means of Transmission	Number of Cases	Percent
Men who have sex with men	6415	62%
Injecting drug use	1227	12%
Men who have sex with men and inject drugs	1037	10%
Heterosexual contact	358	3%
Other	1322	13%
Total	10,359	

Females

Means of Transmission	Number of Cases	Percent
Injecting drug use	929	33%
Heterosexual contact	1401	50%
Other	452	16%
Total	2782	

Source: Centers for Disease Control and Prevention.

Cobb, *Adolescence, Continuity, Change, and Diversity*, Second Edition, ©1995 Mayfield Publishing Company

51 Leading Causes of Death Among Males (top) and Females (bottom) 25–44 Years of Age—United States, 1980–1989

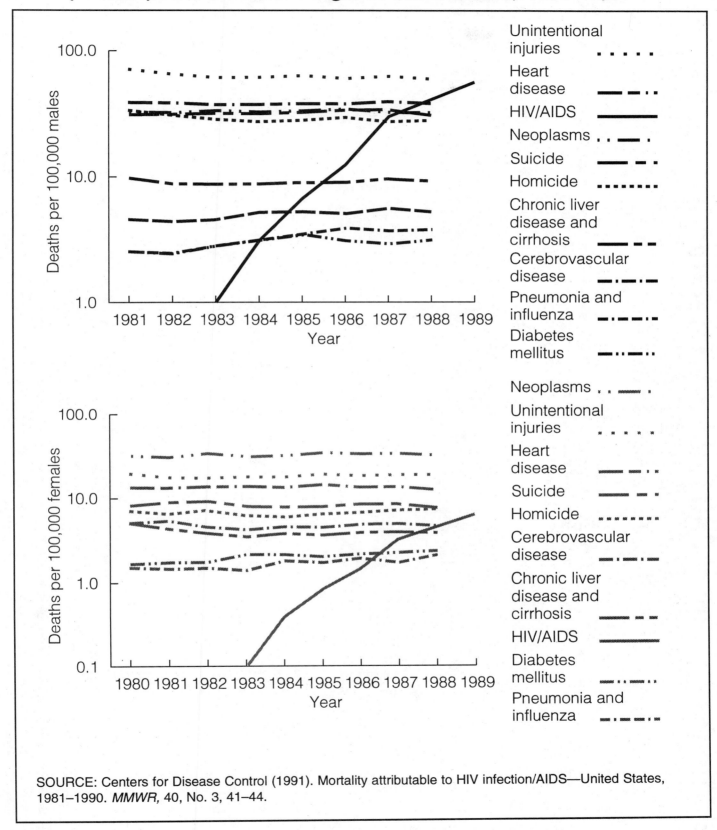

Legend (top, males):
Unintentional injuries
Heart disease
HIV/AIDS
Neoplasms
Suicide
Homicide
Chronic liver disease and cirrhosis
Cerebrovascular disease
Pneumonia and influenza
Diabetes mellitus

Legend (bottom, females):
Neoplasms
Unintentional injuries
Heart disease
Suicide
Homicide
Cerebrovascular disease
Chronic liver disease and cirrhosis
HIV/AIDS
Diabetes mellitus
Pneumonia and influenza

SOURCE: Centers for Disease Control (1991). Mortality attributable to HIV infection/AIDS—United States, 1981–1990. *MMWR*, 40, No. 3, 41–44.

52 The Progressive Cause of HIV Infection

Early Phase

Infection with HIV

HIV is transmitted through intimate contact with body fluids—blood, blood products, semen, or vaginal secretions. The primary means of transmission are sexual contact, direct exposure to blood through injecting drug use or transfusions (prior to 1985), and from an infected mother to her child during pregnancy, childbirth, or breastfeeding.

The body produces antibodies to HIV (seroconversion)

Antibodies usually appear 2 to 12 weeks after the initial infection, a process known as seroconversion. Once antibodies appear, an infected person tests positive if given an HIV-antibody test. About 30 percent of people experience flulike symptoms during this period, lasting for a few days to a few weeks.

Immune system decline

Though the individual has no symptoms, the virus is infecting and destroying cells of the immune system. Many people remain asymptomatic for 3 to 10 or more years. About half of all people infected with HIV develop AIDS within 10 years.

Intermediate Phase

Mild to moderate symptoms

Once the immune system is damaged, many people begin to experience symptoms such as skin rashes, fatigue, weight loss, night sweats, and so on. When the damage is more severe, people are vulnerable to opportunistic infections. Treatments may allow recovery, but infections often recur.

Advanced Phase

AIDS: Severe symptoms and opportunistic infections; immune system failure; death

People are diagnosed with AIDS if they develop one of the conditions defined as a marker for AIDS or if their CD4 lymphocyte count drops below 200/mm³. Chronic or recurrent illnesses continue until the immune system fails and death results.

SOURCE: B. Strong and C. DeVault (1994). *Human Sexuality.* Mountain View, CA: Mayfield.

53 Unemployment among White and Minority Youth

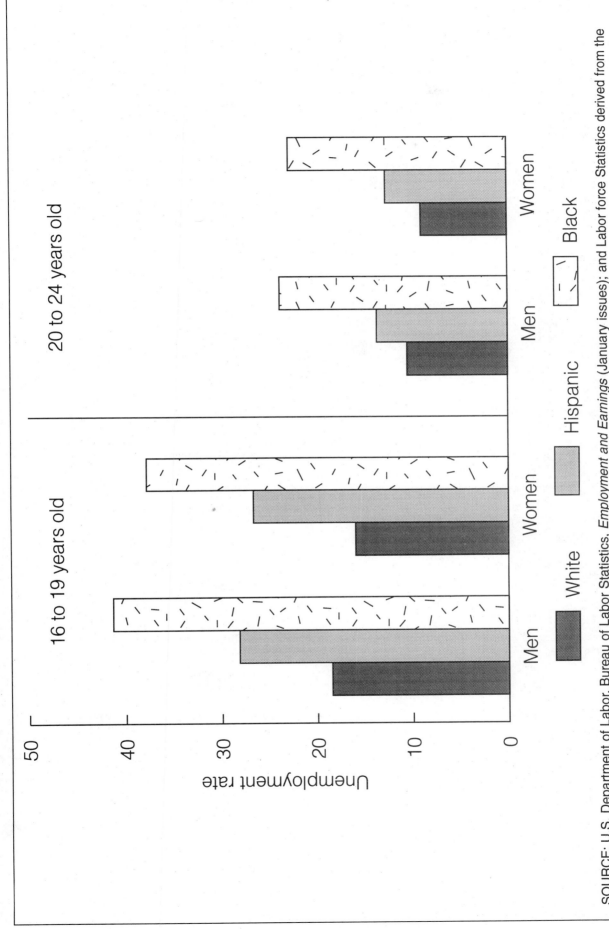

SOURCE: U.S. Department of Labor, Bureau of Labor Statistics, *Employment and Earnings* (January issues); and Labor force Statistics derived from the *Current Population Survey: A Data Book*, vol. 1, Bulletin 2096. In Youth Indicators (1991). *Trends in the well-being of American youth*. Washington, D.C.: U.S. Government Printing Office.

54 How High School Seniors Spend Their Money

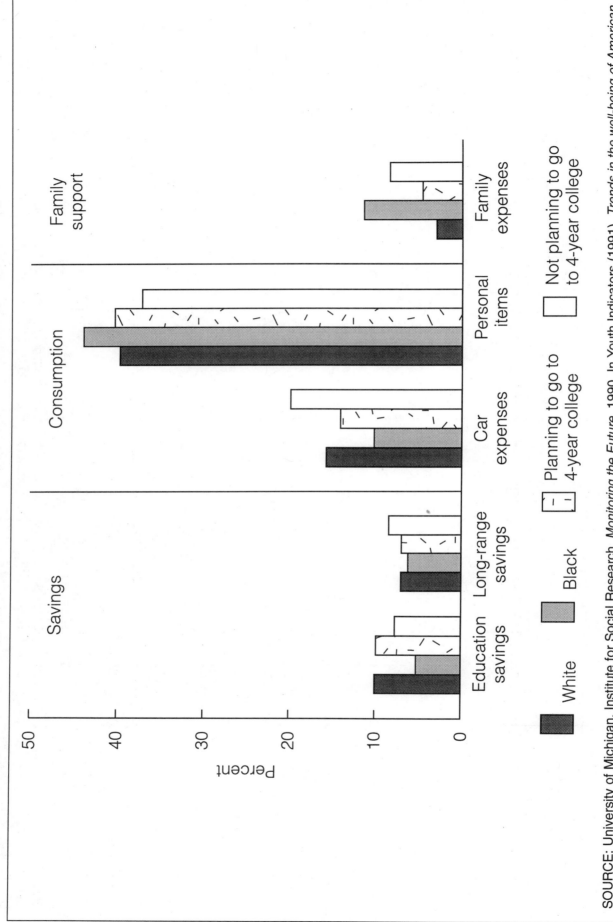

SOURCE: University of Michigan, Institute for Social Research, *Monitoring the Future*, 1990. In Youth Indicators (1991). *Trends in the well-being of American youth*. Washington, D.C.: U.S. Government Printing Office.

Cobb, *Adolescence, Continuity, Change, and Diversity*, Second Edition, © 1995 Mayfield Publishing Company

55 Occupations and Median Weekly Earnings of Males and Females, 1992

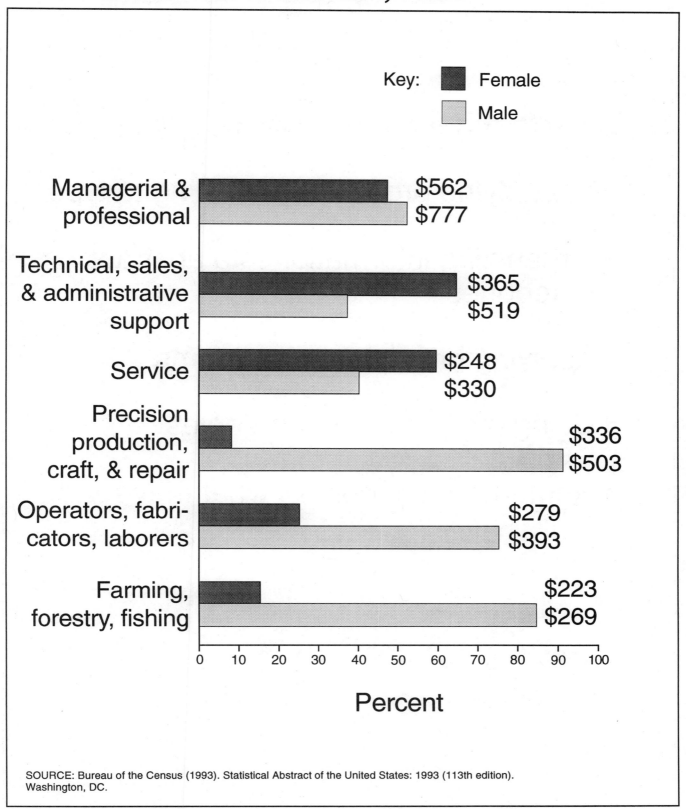

Key: ■ Female □ Male

Occupation	Female	Male
Managerial & professional	$562	$777
Technical, sales, & administrative support	$365	$519
Service	$248	$330
Precision production, craft, & repair	$336	$503
Operators, fabricators, laborers	$279	$393
Farming, forestry, fishing	$223	$269

Percent

SOURCE: Bureau of the Census (1993). Statistical Abstract of the United States: 1993 (113th edition). Washington, DC.

Experts differ from novices by:

- Classifying problems according to type

- Organizing information into abstract categories

- Applying principles to problems

- Using more efficient strategies

- Remembering more of what they read

- High tolerance for ambiguity

- Ability to bend the rules when necessary

- Analytic and intuitive

- Open-minded

- Reflective and spontaneous

Cobb, *Adolescence, Continuity, Change, and Diversity,* Second Edition, ©1995 Mayfield Publishing Company

Dualism: Looking for Answers
Operates within a single frame of reference
Views facts as either right or wrong
Approaches problems by looking for the right answer
Thinks of learning as the accumulation of facts

Relativism: Losing Oneself to Ideas
Aware of more than one frame of reference
Views facts as interpretations that make sense within one, but not necessarily all, frames of reference
Compares ideas instead of looking for the one that is right
Thinks of learning as the evaluation of ideas

Commitment to Relativism: Finding Oneself
Commitment to a particular point of view
Views facts as having meaning within that perspective
Compares ideas in terms of their personal relevance
Thinks of learning in terms of what one experiences through committing oneself to a course of action

Cobb, *Adolescence, Continuity, Change, and Diversity,* Second Edition, ©1995 Mayfield Publishing Company

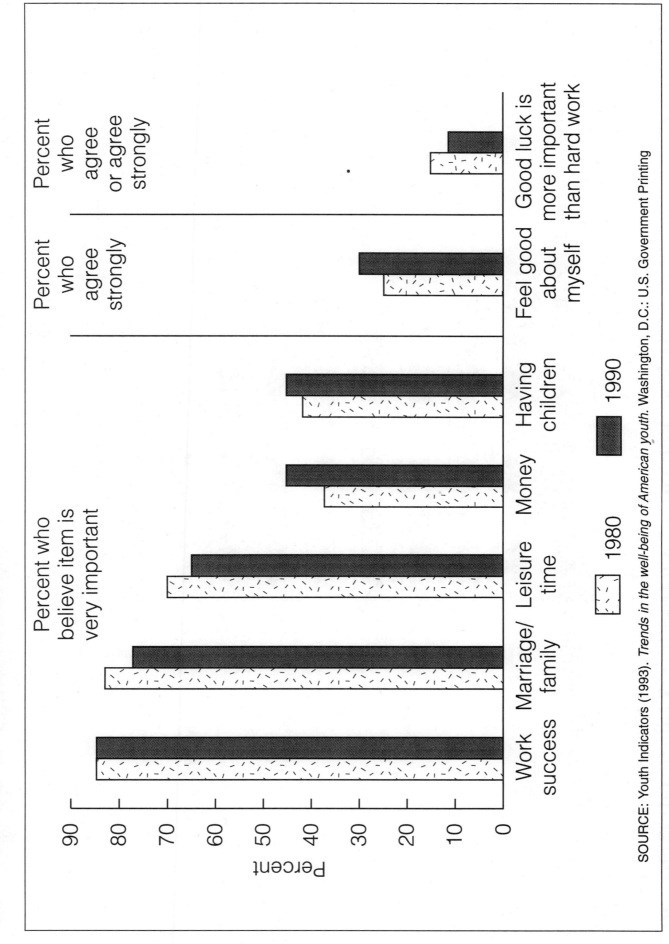

SOURCE: Youth Indicators (1993). *Trends in the well-being of American youth.* Washington, D.C.: U.S. Government Printing

Cobb, *Adolescence, Continuity, Change, and Diversity,* Second Edition, © 1995 Mayfield Publishing Company

Percent of High School Seniors Indicating that They Agree with Their Parents on Selected Topics: 1975 and 1991

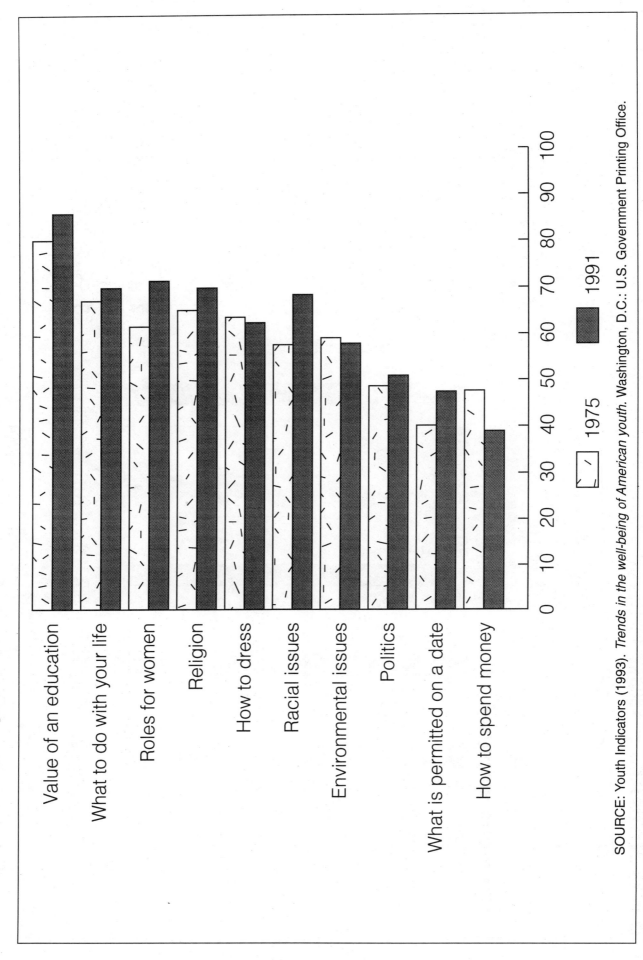

SOURCE: Youth Indicators (1993). *Trends in the well-being of American youth.* Washington, D.C.: U.S. Government Printing Office.

Cobb, *Adolescence, Continuity, Change, and Diversity,* Second Edition, © 1995 Mayfield Publishing Company

61 Religious Practices and Beliefs Among High School Seniors: 1976 to 1991

Percent of seniors

Religious activity & level of interest	'76	'78	'80	'82	'84	'85	'86	'87	'88	'89	'90	'91
Frequency of attending religious services												
Weekly	40.7	39.4	43.1	37.7	37.7	35.3	34.3	31.8	31.9	31.4	30.4	31.2
1-2 times a month	16.3	17.2	16.3	17.4	16.2	16.6	16.8	15.6	17.3	16.6	15.7	16.8
Rarely	32.0	34.4	32.0	35.8	35.8	37.0	36.9	39.6	39.0	38.5	39.7	37.6
Never	11.0	9.0	8.6	9.6	10.2	11.1	12.0	13.0	11.7	13.5	14.1	14.4
Importance of religion in life												
Very important	28.8	27.8	32.4	28.4	29.7	27.3	26.3	24.9	26.1	27.2	26.4	27.7
Pretty important	30.5	33.0	32.6	33.0	32.6	32.4	32.7	31.7	31.9	30.3	29.5	30.0
A little	27.8	27.9	25.3	27.9	26.7	27.6	27.8	28.8	28.4	27.8	28.7	27.0
Not important	12.9	11.2	9.8	10.7	11.0	12.7	13.3	14.5	13.6	14.7	15.5	15.3

SOURCE: Youth Indicators. (1993). *Trends in the well-being of American youth.* Washington, DC: U.S. Government Printing Office.

Cobb, *Adolescence, Continuity, Change, and Diversity,* Second Edition, ©1995 Mayfield Publishing Company

Frequency of Positive Outcomes Following the Death of a Loved One, by Locus of Control Orientation Among Late Adolescents

Positive Outcomes	Locus of Control Orientation	
	Low External (n = 44)	High External (n = 49)
Have deeper appreciation of life	66%	82%
Show greater caring for loved ones	59%	74%
Strengthened emotional bonds with others	61%	51%
Developed emotional strength	55%	51%
Increased empathy for others	48%	47%
Better communication skills	39%	18%*
Enhanced problem solving skills	11%	6%

* p < .05.

SOURCE: Oltjenbruns, K.A. (1991). Positive outcomes of adolescents' experience with grief. *Journal of Adolescent Research, 6*, 43–53. ©1991 by Sage Publications. Reprinted by permission of Sage Publications, Inc.

63 Long-term Physical Consequences of Childhood Abuse (Physical, Emotional, and/or Sexual)

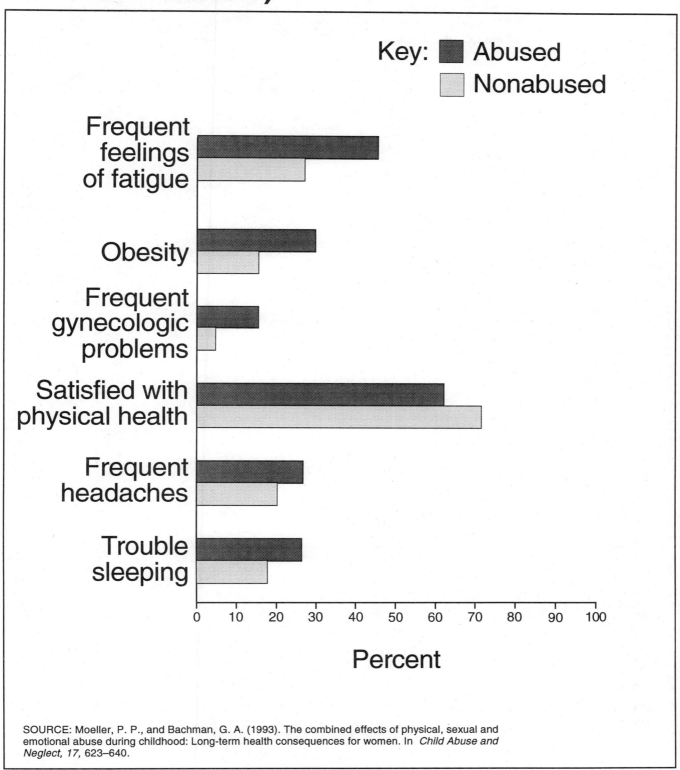

Key: ■ Abused □ Nonabused

Frequent feelings of fatigue

Obesity

Frequent gynecologic problems

Satisfied with physical health

Frequent headaches

Trouble sleeping

0 10 20 30 40 50 60 70 80 90 100

Percent

SOURCE: Moeller, P. P., and Bachman, G. A. (1993). The combined effects of physical, sexual and emotional abuse during childhood: Long-term health consequences for women. In *Child Abuse and Neglect, 17*, 623–640.

64 Percentage of High School Seniors Reporting Ever Having Used Drugs

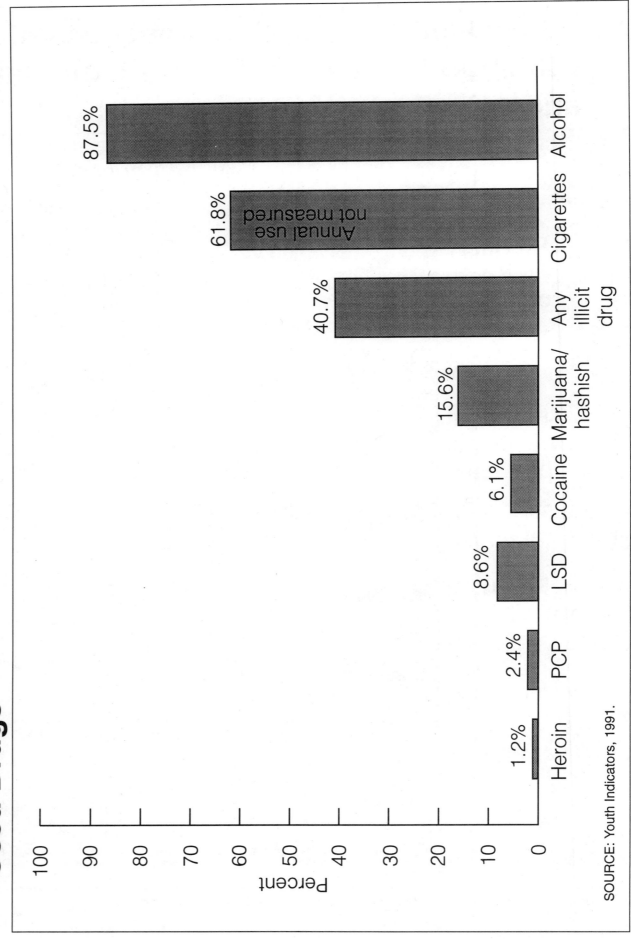

SOURCE: Youth Indicators, 1991.

Cobb, *Adolescence, Continuity, Change, and Diversity*, Second Edition, © 1995 Mayfield Publishing Company

65 Adolescents' Attitudes Toward Drug Use

Percentage of Adolescents Judging Item as "Not All Right" in Interview

Interview Question	Grade[a]			
	10	11	12	$\overline{X}$
All right to use illegal drugs?	65	60	70	65
All right to use illegal drug which has positive physical effects?	40	65	50	52
All right to use legal drug which has negative physical effects?	75	75	65	72
All right to use illegal drug which has positive psychological effects?	55	60	65	60
All right to use legal drug which has negative psychological effects?	80	60	80	73
All right to use illegal drugs in other places if legal?	65	55	30	50
All right to use legal drugs here?	35	35	20	30
All right for government to prohibit?	10	5	5	7
All right for parents to prohibit in the home?	0	0	0	0
Parents to prohibit outside the home?	25	20	15	20
Religious authorities to prohibit?	35	50	35	40
Do people have right to harm themselves?	5	35	35	25
Have the right to kill themselves?	15	60	50	42
The right to harm self if negative consequences for others?	70	85	55	70

a. N = 60

SOURCE: Killen, M., Leviton, M., and Cahill, J. (1991). Adolescent reasoning about drug use. *Journal of Adolescent Research, 6,* 336–356. ©1991 by Sage Publications. Reprinted by permission of Sage Publications, Inc.

Percentage of Female and Male High School Students Reporting Suicidal Thoughts and Behavior

	Suicidal Thoughts	Made Suicide Plans	One or More Suicide Attempts	Attempt(s) Requiring Medical Attention
Females	37	25	11	2
Males	21	13	4	1
Total	29	19	7	2

SOURCE: U.S. Department of Health and Human Services, Centers for Disease Control. Behaviors Related to Unintentional and Intentional Injuries Among High School Students—United States, 1991. *Morbidity and Mortality Weekly Report*, Oct. 16, 1992. Washington, DC: U.S. Government Printing Office.

Coping strategy:	Social/Peer Stress		School/Academic Stress	
	$\overline{X}$[b]	SD	$\overline{X}$	SD
Problem-focused	26.7	4.0	27.5	3.8
Wishful thinking	12.0	2.7	11.6	2.3
Detachment	15.2	3.7	13.5	3.6
Seeking support	18.1	3.5	17.5	3.4
Focus of the positive	9.7	2.1	10.4	2.3
Self-blame	7.4	1.8	8.9	2.2
Tension reduction	3.1	1.4	3.1	1.4
Keep to self	7.8	2.5	7.4	7.1
Anger arousal	27.5	7.7	24.5	6.6

b. Means expressed in terms of percentage of total coping efforts exerted.

SOURCE: K.E. (1991). Coping with anger-provoking situations: Adolescent coping in relation to anger reactivity. *Journal of Adolescent Research, 6*, 357–370. ©1991 by Sage Publications. Reprinted by permission of Sage Publications, Inc.

68 Types of Relationships Found in Research

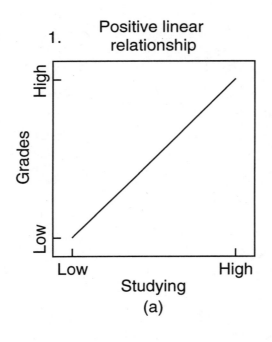

1. Positive linear relationship

(a)

Grades (y-axis: Low to High)
Studying (x-axis: Low to High)

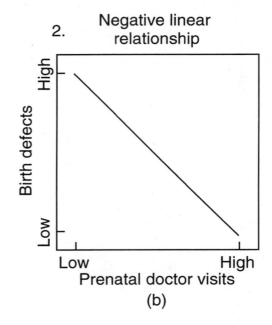

2. Negative linear relationship

(b)

Birth defects (y-axis: Low to High)
Prenatal doctor visits (x-axis: Low to High)

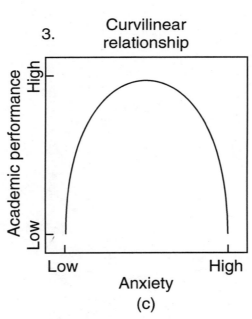

3. Curvilinear relationship

(c)

Academic performance (y-axis: Low to High)
Anxiety (x-axis: Low to High)

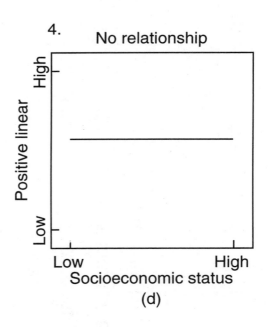

4. No relationship

(d)

Positive linear (y-axis: Low to High)
Socioeconomic status (x-axis: Low to High)

SOURCE: Cozby, Worden, Kee. 1989. *Research Methods in Human Development*, p. 32.

Cohort (year of birth)	1970	1975	1980	1985	1990
1960	1 10	2 15	3 20	4	5
1965	6	7 10	8 15	9 20	10
1970	11	12	13 10	14 15	15 20

Time of measurement

A Sequential Design
The cells are numbered in the upper-right hand corner. The numbers in the centers of the cells are ages.